JANUARY 2017

Reinvigorating U.S. Economic Strategy in the Asia Pacific

Recommendations for the Incoming Administration

COMMISSION COCHAIRS
Charlene Barshefsky
Evan G. Greenberg
Jon M. Huntsman Jr.

A REPORT OF THE
CSIS ASIA ECONOMIC STRATEGY COMMISSION

CSIS | CENTER FOR STRATEGIC & INTERNATIONAL STUDIES

ROWMAN &
LITTLEFIELD
Lanham • Boulder • New York • London

About CSIS

For over 50 years, the Center for Strategic and International Studies (CSIS) has worked to develop solutions to the world's greatest policy challenges. Today, CSIS scholars are providing strategic insights and bipartisan policy solutions to help decisionmakers chart a course toward a better world.

CSIS is a nonprofit organization headquartered in Washington, D.C. The Center's 220 full-time staff and large network of affiliated scholars conduct research and analysis and develop policy initiatives that look into the future and anticipate change.

Founded at the height of the Cold War by David M. Abshire and Admiral Arleigh Burke, CSIS was dedicated to finding ways to sustain American prominence and prosperity as a force for good in the world. Since 1962, CSIS has become one of the world's preeminent international institutions focused on defense and security; regional stability; and transnational challenges ranging from energy and climate to global health and economic integration.

Thomas J. Pritzker was named chairman of the CSIS Board of Trustees in November 2015. Former U.S. deputy secretary of defense John J. Hamre has served as the Center's president and chief executive officer since 2000.

CSIS does not take specific policy positions; accordingly, all views expressed herein should be understood to be solely those of the author(s).

ISBN: 978-1-4422-7976-6 (pb); 978-1-4422-7977-3 (eBook)

Center for Strategic & International Studies
1616 Rhode Island Avenue, NW
Washington, DC 20036
202-887-0200 | www.**csis**.org

Rowman & Littlefield
4501 Forbes Boulevard
Lanham, MD 20706
301-459-3366 | www.**rowman**.com

Contents

The CSIS Asia Economic Strategy Commission

Cochairs	Charlene Barshefsky Evan G. Greenberg Jon M. Huntsman Jr.
Commissioners	Timothy Adams Richard L. Armitage Gary Baumgartner Karan Bhatia Gary Edson Anne Finucane Stephen W. Green Reed Hundt Rod Hunter Charles Lake J. Stapleton Roy Kathleen Stephens Mona Sutphen Christopher Townsend Laura D'Andrea Tyson
Project Directors	Matthew P. Goodman Scott Miller Amy E. Searight

Preface

The Asia Pacific is home to over half of humanity and many of the world's largest and most dynamic economies. Over the coming decades, no region of the world will do more to shape U.S. economic fortunes. More than ever before, American jobs and growth are tied to the Asia Pacific, and these opportunities are likely to grow.

But the region is undergoing profound change. Today, mutually beneficial relations with the Asia Pacific are challenged by slowing growth, a rise in security tensions, and threats to the U.S.-led order. The rise of China is altering the Asia-Pacific landscape in profound ways and playing a critical role in the region's prosperity and perceived stability. These economic and security shifts offer opportunities for the United States to strengthen cooperation with emerging economies and reinforce partnerships with established allies. But new policies are needed in what has become a more volatile environment. These policies must be grounded in the enduring interests of the United States and informed by the realities of a changing Asia Pacific. And just as economics is at the heart of Asia's rise, so must economics be at the heart of an effective strategy.

We convened the CSIS Asia Economic Strategy Commission to help inform such a reinvigorated strategy. In the report that follows, we call on the incoming administration to outline, both for the American people and Asia, a vision for a prosperous and inclusive trans-Pacific economic order.

With confident leadership and energetic execution, we believe such a strategy will help to uphold enduring U.S. interests, advance the peace and prosperity of the Asia Pacific, and build a firm foundation for America's Pacific century.

Charlene Barshefsky
Evan G. Greenberg
Jon M. Huntsman Jr.

Acknowledgments

In September 2015, CSIS launched the Asia Economic Strategy Commission under the leadership of Charlene Barshefsky, Evan Greenberg, and Jon Huntsman. The Commission, made up of 18 national leaders with extensive experience in government, the private sector, nongovernmental organizations, and academia, met formally four times—in September and December 2015, and in May and October 2016. The cochairs and staff directors traveled to Asia for a listening tour in March 2016.

Input from external experts in the United States and from across the Asia Pacific was critical to developing the final report and recommendations. The CSIS project team held roundtables and conducted interviews in Washington, New York, and San Francisco, as well as in Beijing, Jakarta, Seoul, Singapore, and Tokyo. The experts we met with brought a wealth of experience and insight from across the public and private sectors, as well as deep regional expertise. We would like to thank all of these individuals, many of them good friends from across the region, for giving so generously of their time.

A number of CSIS scholars and researchers contributed to the production of this report. Ernest Bower played a critical role in conceptualizing the project and getting it off the ground. Murray Hiebert provided invaluable advice on substance and process throughout. David Parker and Daniel Sofio led the CSIS staff that formed the drafting and research teams. Grace Hearty, Kathleen Rustici, Shannon Hayden, Benjamin Contreras, and Elizabeth Keller provided tireless coordination and administrative support throughout the commission. Phuong Nguyen and Daniel Remler provided vital research and drafting support.

This project was made possible by the generous support of Aflac International Inc.; Bank of America; Chubb Limited and Chubb Group; General Electric; Chevron; MetLife, Inc.; and the Pharmaceutical Research and Manufacturers of America.

All commissioners participated in this effort in an individual capacity, not on behalf of the institutions they represent. The findings of this report reflect a broad consensus of those involved, but individual commissioners do not necessarily endorse every recommendation.

Executive Summary

No region of the world will do more to shape U.S. economic prospects over the coming decades than the Asia Pacific. More of our trade, growth, and jobs than ever are tied to the world's fastest-growing region. But the Asia Pacific is changing in profound ways that will shape our future prosperity and security. To take advantage of the opportunities of a changing Asia Pacific and deal with the challenges there, the incoming administration in Washington will need an effective strategy that advances U.S. interests, has economics at the heart, and begins on day one.

Over the past four decades, the economic size of the Asia Pacific has grown fivefold. By 2030, Asia alone will be home to more than half the world's middle-class consumers. This means opportunity. There will be more demand for the full range of U.S. exports and expertise, from agricultural products to advanced technologies and services. Asia-Pacific countries are already the destination for some 28 percent of U.S. exports and support almost 3.5 million U.S. jobs.

The United States has a robust alliance system and deep economic ties with the region. Demand for American leadership is strong: the queue of countries eager to join the Trans-Pacific Partnership (TPP) is a clear indication of the appeal of U.S.-led initiatives. We can build on these advantages. Our partnerships with established allies, such as Japan and Korea, are dynamic and poised to deepen. Our cooperation with newer partners, such as India and the 10 countries of the Association of Southeast Asian Nations (ASEAN), is ripe for growth.

However, the U.S. position in the region is also facing new challenges. Growth is slowing, nationalism is rising, and countries are vying for regional leadership. China's growth has created enormous opportunities for U.S. exporters and investment, but slowing growth, stalled reforms, and mercantilist policies are creating a far more difficult environment for U.S. companies in China. From laying down airstrips in the South China Sea to building roads and railways across Central Asia, Beijing is using its newfound might to assert influence across the region in ways that change U.S. leadership there.

The United States benefits from a cooperative U.S.-China relationship, but a positive relationship cannot be sustained if it does not advance the interests of both countries. Washington must be willing to work with Beijing, but also to hold China accountable. This means challenging Beijing where it seeks to undermine the rules-based order or when its actions threaten U.S. interests. It also means broad and consistent involvement in the region to preserve and enhance U.S. interests.

The last eight U.S. presidents have recognized the importance of the Asia Pacific. Administrations from both sides of the aisle have done many things right to take advantage of opportunities and reduce risks in the region.

But today's changing Asia Pacific demands a revitalized U.S. economic strategy. It must be built around a few core objectives that best serve U.S. interests, including open, rules-based markets; a trans-Pacific order supported by transparent institutions and rules; and peace and stability. The strategy must also respond to the needs and realities of Asia. A strategy that demands the region choose between the United States and China will fail.

To assist the new U.S. administration taking office on January 20, 2017, the bipartisan CSIS Asia Economic Strategy Commission has put forward the outlines of such a strategy, with eight topline policy recommendations.

We begin with two caveats. First, an effective international economic strategy starts at home. The next administration must take action to support strong and inclusive U.S. growth. Among other measures, this means investing in infrastructure, education, training, and innovation. It means fixing our tax code and our regulatory system. Absent appropriate domestic reforms, global competition will erode U.S. economic leadership, undermine our national security, and weaken domestic support for our involvement in the world.

Second, effective U.S. strategy is not only about tools and tactics; it also requires the right mindset. The next administration must start and end with a confident assertion of U.S. interests and understand the fundamental role of economics in Asia-Pacific political and security affairs. It must be willing to both encourage countries to follow the U.S. lead, and to respond to actions that are inconsistent with U.S. interests. It must embrace coalition building, working with allies and partners in the region, as well as mobilizing and supporting the U.S. private sector. And it must develop effective messages that explain the importance of the Asia Pacific to the American people and build support in the region for continued U.S. leadership there.

The authors of this report believe that a well-conceived and energetically executed strategy toward the vital Asia-Pacific region is not only worth an investment of time, resources, and political capital by the new administration; it is essential to long-term U.S. prosperity and security.

RECOMMENDATIONS

1. *Articulate a clear vision of the United States as a Pacific power*: Starting with the inaugural speech, the new president should make clear to the American people, in words and policies, that the United States is a Pacific power and that robust trans-Pacific exchange is critical to our future prosperity and security.

2. *Complete TPP, and continue working to open markets and strengthen rules in the Asia Pacific*: Ratification of TPP—fixed as needed—is critical to U.S. credibility in Asia and to our role as champion of a rules-based order following Western norms. The new administration should work toward its eventual passage and in the meantime continue to promote liberalization and high-standard rules like those in TPP.
3. *Take action to ensure that the U.S.-China relationship is mutually beneficial*: A mutually beneficial U.S.-China economic relationship is strongly in U.S. interests. However, the relationship is currently out of balance. The new administration should continue to pursue cooperation with Beijing where possible, while responding forcefully to Chinese practices that harm U.S. interests.
4. *Take action to maintain U.S. technological leadership*: America's comparative advantage in technology is vital to our prosperity and security. In addition to making the right investments in innovation at home, the new administration must work to ensure high, open standards for technology internationally and protect U.S. intellectual property.
5. *Bring U.S. strengths to the infrastructure push across Asia*: Washington needs a more coherent strategy for U.S. involvement in the current infrastructure investment push across Asia. The strategy should be built around U.S. strengths, including commitment to the rule of law, transparency, and world-leading companies.
6. *Update and uphold the Asia-Pacific economic architecture*: The new administration should work with partner countries and the private sector to strengthen and streamline economic institutions that support a rules-based order in the Asia Pacific, such the Asian Development Bank (ADB) and the Asia-Pacific Economic Cooperation (APEC) forum. It should also participate more fully in the economic dimensions of ASEAN cooperation.
7. *Work with Congress to rebuild U.S. leverage and fully resource U.S. priorities in Asia*: The new administration should assess the adequacy of current spending to support U.S. economic priorities in the Asia Pacific and identify where additional investments are needed, review measures available under current law to address unfair economic policies, and work with Congress to enhance U.S. resources and leverage.
8. *Build an effective interagency Asia economic team coordinated by the White House*: The new administration should update its policymaking apparatus to reflect the critical importance of economic tools in a comprehensive strategy toward the Asia region, and improve coordination across the U.S. government and with stakeholders.

01

Introduction

Asked why he robbed banks, Willie Sutton reportedly said, "Because that's where the money is." The same logic has drawn the United States to the Asia Pacific for over 200 years. The region today holds more than half the world's trillion-dollar economies, and by 2030, it will be home to more than half the world's middle-class consumers.[1] More U.S. trade, growth, and jobs than ever are tied to the region, and our future prosperity depends on staying actively involved there.

But the Asia Pacific is changing in profound ways that may not always favor U.S. interests. Growth is slowing, nationalism is rising, and countries are vying for regional leadership. The incoming administration in Washington needs to address these changes and have an effective strategy that advances U.S. interests, has economics at the heart, and begins on day one.

The United States is a Pacific power. Our economic and security interests in the region have long been intertwined. Even before the American republic was founded, a merchant ship carrying furs and ginseng sailed from New York to Canton in 1784, and the man in charge of the cargo stayed on as our first consul there. American "black ships" arrived in Japan in 1853 to open the country to trade. Over the past 75 years, the United States has built alliances that today form the bedrock of security in the Asia Pacific. The stability this has provided has enabled Asia's rapid growth and integration, contributing to an enormous expansion in trans-Pacific economic ties. This investment has paid enormous dividends for the United States, expanding economic opportunities at home and reinforcing U.S. security.

Just as economics has been fundamental to our involvement in the Asia Pacific since the beginning, it is still what draws us there today. The economies of Asia—first Japan, then "Asian tigers" like South Korea, Taiwan, and Singapore, and now China, India, and others—have pulled the global center of economic gravity toward the Asia Pacific. Over the past four decades, the region's

---

1. Cheng Li, *China's Emerging Middle Class: Beyond Economic Transformation* (Washington, DC: Brookings Institution Press, 2010).

economic size has grown fivefold. By 2030, Asia will account for more than 40 percent of global gross domestic product (GDP).[2]

This means more demand for the full range of U.S. exports and expertise: meat, grains, and produce; automobiles, capital equipment, and energy; health care, financial services, and computer software. Asia-Pacific countries are already the destination for some 28 percent of U.S. exports and support almost 3.5 million U.S. jobs, and these figures are likely to grow.[3]

The benefits of our economic ties with Asia are clearly visible in states and cities across the United States. For the Pacific-facing states, Asia is the single-largest destination for exports of goods and services. Colorado sends more than $1 billion in semiconductors across the Pacific and sells over $3 billion in services to Asians.[4] In midwestern states, economic ties with Asia are growing rapidly; Missouri, for example, has seen exports to the region grow almost 500 percent over the past decade, led by trade in agricultural goods. In the South and on the East Coast, trade with Asia accounts for more than 30 percent of all export-related jobs in states such as Georgia and Massachusetts.[5]

Inbound investment from Asia is also growing, creating growth and jobs for Americans. As of 2015, the stock of Asia-sourced direct investment in the United States was more than $550 billion.[6] Japanese and other foreign-owned factories and offices operating in the United States directly employ more than one million Americans, with many more jobs supported indirectly by these operations.[7] Chinese investment in the United States has been growing rapidly, with three times as many new deals in the first half of 2016 as in the same period of 2015.[8] This will help create American jobs.

However, we cannot take this mutually advantageous future for granted. Economic opportunity in the Asia Pacific is threatened by a combination of slowing growth, rising nationalism, and creeping protectionism. Competition is intensifying. China and others are asserting regional leadership and challenging the U.S.-led order. Active, consistent policy involvement by Washington is essential to preserve and extend the benefits of U.S. economic and security ties with Asia.

---

2. Asian Development Bank (ADB), *Asia 2050: Realizing the Asian Century: Executive Summary* (Manila: ADB, August 2011), https://www.adb.org/publications/asia-2050-realizing-asian-century.

3. Chris Rasmussen and Susan Xu, "Jobs Supported by Export Destination 2015," Office of Trade and Economic Analysis, September 2016, http://www.trade.gov/mas/ian/build/groups/public/@tg_ian/documents/webcontent/tg_ian_005508.pdf.

4. Asia Matters for America, "Colorado and Asia: Highlights," East-West Center, accessed October 2016, http://www.asiamattersforamerica.org/sites/default/files//pdfs/AsiaMattersforAmerica_Colorado.pdf.

5. Asia Matters for America, "U.S.-Asia Interactions in Georgia State and Congressional Districts," East-West Center, accessed October 2016, http://www.asiamattersforamerica.org/georgia.

6. Bureau of Economic Analysis (BEA), "Direct Investment and Multinational Enterprises, Foreign Direct Investment Position in the United States on a Historical-Cost Basis," U.S. Department of Commerce, accessed October 2016, http://www.bea.gov/iTable/index_MNC.cfm.

7. Organization for International Investment, "Insourcing Facts," August 2016, http://www.ofii.org/resources/insourcing-facts.

8. Thilo Hanemann and Cassie Gao, "Chinese FDI in the U.S.: Tripling Down on America," Rhodium Group, July 22, 2016, http://rhg.com/notes/chinese-fdi-in-the-us-tripling-down-on-america.

We have a robust system of alliances in the region, but many of these countries—notably Japan and South Korea—are struggling to generate strong, sustained growth. Countries from India to Indonesia continue to pursue protectionist policies that limit opportunities for U.S. exporters and investors. And Washington has yet to tap the full potential of its ties with the Association of Southeast Asian Nations (ASEAN), a $2.4 trillion economic area and home to more than 600 million potential customers for U.S. products and services, but one also facing its own growth and governance challenges.

China's emergence as the world's second-largest economy and a regional power presents special opportunities and challenges for the United States. China still has tremendous room for growth and is on track to becoming the world's largest consumer market, offering enormous potential opportunities for U.S. exporters and investors.

But the Chinese economy is slowing as the limits of the old model of investment- and export-led growth are reached. This has both reduced an important source of demand for the global economy and created significant new financial risks. Moreover, in recent years Beijing has backed away from domestic economic reform and created a far more difficult environment for market access and foreign investment in China. At the same time, Beijing is using its newfound economic power to assert its influence in the region, from building military airstrips on reclaimed islands in the disputed South China Sea to offering financial incentives to its neighbors that create a system of economic dependency.

Managing relations with China will require the incoming administration to pursue a clear-eyed strategy that involves elements of both cooperation and competition. Washington should recognize China's vital economic role in the region and try to build a mutually beneficial relationship. But we also need to sharply define, articulate, and defend our interests, and those of our allies, and challenge Beijing where it seeks to broadly undermine the rules-based order or pursues its own interests at the expense of others in the region. We cannot allow a power vacuum to emerge in the Asia Pacific that China alone fills.

The good news is that there remains strong demand for U.S. involvement in Asia. The queue of countries, from Korea to Indonesia, that expressed interest in joining the Trans-Pacific Partnership (TPP) after it was completed in the fall of 2015 is a clear indication of the appeal of U.S.-led initiatives. Many Asians also admire U.S. values, including our commitment to the rule of law and democratic processes. They may not always like U.S. hectoring about norms and standards, preferring to proceed in an "Asian way," but most governments in the region know that strong rules support their own progress. Meanwhile, the combination of China's recent economic slowdown and Beijing's greater assertiveness has troubled neighboring countries; they are wary of overdependence and eager for the United States to play an active counterbalancing role.

The desire for continued American leadership in the region is a unique asset for the United States that should be strategically deployed. Reinforcing our military presence and commitment in the Asia Pacific is necessary for both our security and prosperity, since the latter depends on stability. But too much emphasis on military engagement makes many in Asia uncomfortable; they also want the United States deeply involved in the region's economic affairs, taking a balanced and measured course.

Moreover, countries in Asia do not want to be forced to choose between the United States and China, and Washington should be careful not to suggest this. Thus Washington needs to put forward a vision for a prosperous and inclusive Asia Pacific that benefits all. This vision should be built around several core objectives that best serve U.S. interests, including open, rules-based markets; a trans-Pacific order supported by transparent institutions and rules; and peace and stability.

To their credit, the last eight U.S. presidents, from Richard Nixon through Barack Obama, have recognized the importance of the Asia Pacific. From the opening to China to the "rebalance" strategy, administrations from both sides of the aisle have done many things right to take advantage of opportunities and reduce risks in the region. They have shown up, invested in security and economic initiatives that underpin regional peace and stability and advance liberal norms, and worked to pull China and other formerly isolated countries into the global rules-based order.

But for the past 15 years, Washington has been distracted and inconsistent in its approach to Asia, while realities on the ground have not stood still. Recent policy initiatives, notably TPP, have too often been left to languish. In some cases, such as the initial response to China's proposed Asian Infrastructure Investment Bank (AIIB), Washington has not shown enough recognition of Asians' desire for greater ownership of international institutions. And there has been too little effort to explain the importance of the Asia Pacific to the American people.

The new U.S. administration has an opportunity to address these shortcomings and put into place a reinvigorated Asia strategy with specific new policies to carry it out.

Job one is to do the things at home that are necessary to support America's growth and competitiveness, including investing in infrastructure, education and training, and innovation. As the global economy has expanded and myriad new players have emerged, U.S. competitive prowess cannot be taken for granted. Indeed, absent appropriate domestic policy measures, U.S. economic leadership will erode. There is no substitute for job one.

Ratifying TPP—fixed as needed—is also critical to a successful Asia strategy. Failure of TPP would not only deny the United States economic benefits but also be a severe blow to U.S. credibility and leadership in the region. It would translate into a diminished American role in establishing rules and norms that will govern the twenty-first-century economy, undermining U.S. competitiveness and economic success. It would even raise questions in Asia about the sustainability of our military presence in the region.

To be sure, TPP was at the center of a heated political debate about trade and globalization in the 2016 presidential election year. This is understandable. Washington needs to do a better job of explaining to all Americans the broad benefits of trade and helping workers cope with the dislocations of technological progress, globalization, and other economic changes. But none of this is a reason to jettison—rather than fix—TPP or to pursue policies that are politically expedient but ultimately self-defeating. If America abandons its commitments to openness, transparency, and rules-based action, we should not be surprised when other countries follow suit, to our absolute disadvantage.

The new administration should also draw lessons from the powerful effect TPP has had in incentivizing countries in the region to work with the United States in building a stronger and broader rules-based order. Countries want leadership from Washington, and this can and should be extended to other areas of economic policy. For example, there is a major push under way to build infrastructure across Asia, with China, Japan, and others each announcing its own vision for the region. The United States could contribute more in this area by advocating for high standards and transparency in infrastructure investment and mobilizing the operational and financial expertise of our world-leading companies. We can and must exert similar leadership in promoting high standards and legal protections in the areas of innovation and technology, which are critical to our long-term economic success.

An effective Asia strategy is not just a matter of updating the U.S. government's policy toolkit. It also requires the right mindset, one that starts and ends with confident assertion of U.S. interests and is based on an understanding of the fundamental role that economics plays in Asia-Pacific political and security affairs. There must be a willingness not only to entice countries to follow the U.S. lead, but also to respond to actions adverse to our interests. At the same time, we need to do more to recognize Asians' desire for greater leadership in regional and global economic affairs; this includes broadening representation in existing institutions to reflect today's economic reality and considering U.S. participation in the AIIB.

A successful strategy requires Washington to work more closely with our treaty allies in the region, particularly Australia, Japan, and South Korea. Countries from Singapore to India are also vital partners. In all its work in Asia, Washington also needs to both mobilize and support the private sector—the sharp end of the spear of our economic involvement in Asia. And the administration must develop effective messages that explain the importance of the Asia Pacific to the American people and build support in the region for continued U.S. leadership there.

The approach described here is a tall order for any administration, given the inevitable press of other business both at home and abroad. But Asia is critical and must remain a priority in the years ahead. The authors of this report strongly believe that a well-conceived and energetically executed strategy in the Asia Pacific is not only worth the investment of time, resources, and political capital; it is essential to long-term U.S. prosperity and security.

BOX 1.1.

The "Asia Pacific" in its general use here includes the 18 countries of the East Asia Summit (EAS)—that is, the 10 members of the Association of Southeast Asian Nations (Brunei, Cambodia, Indonesia, Laos, Malaysia, Burma, the Philippines, Singapore, Thailand, Vietnam), plus Australia, China, India, Japan, New Zealand, the Republic of Korea, the United States, and Russia. Other countries of the region are mentioned where appropriate.

This report covers broad Asia strategy. As such, its focus is regional, dealing with individual economies as appropriate. However, given the nature of U.S. interests and the structure of the U.S. government, the authors recognize that the new administration will also need specific strategies toward the key economies of the region. These include China, Japan, India, South Korea, Australia, Taiwan, and the ASEAN nations. CSIS intends to provide specific recommendations on these bilateral strategies as the new administration gears up its work on the Asia Pacific.

02

The Asia-Pacific Landscape

The Asia Pacific is the world's most dynamic economic region. It holds enormous potential for growth and increased prosperity, including for U.S. businesses, workers, and consumers. At the same time, as a result of shifting economic and security conditions, the region faces greater change and uncertainty than at perhaps any other time in the past quarter century. The ability of the next administration to develop and execute an effective U.S. strategy toward the Asia Pacific requires a thorough understanding of these evolving dynamics.

ASIA'S ECONOMIC POTENTIAL

Today the economies of the Asia-Pacific region produce more than half of global economic output; their combined GDP is more than $40 trillion. Over the past decade, average annual growth in GDP per capita across the APEC region has been more than a percentage point above the global average.[1] Over the same period, the region as a whole has accounted for more than half of global GDP growth. U.S. prosperity and security are increasingly tied to the economic success of the Asia Pacific.

In an August 2011 report, the ADB illustrated Asia's long-term potential by estimating what would happen if the region maintained its recent trajectory through 2050.[2] Over this time frame, the size of Asia's urban population would rise from 1.6 to 3 billion. The region would see its share of global GDP nearly double, rising to more than 50 percent of the world total. Measured at market exchange rates, Asia's GDP would increase more than 10-fold, from $17 trillion in 2011 to more than $170 trillion. On a purchasing power parity (PPP) basis, GDP per capita would exceed $40,000, making the average Asian citizen in 2050 richer than the average citizen in Japan or South Korea today.

---

1. Asia-Pacific Economic Cooperation (APEC), "APEC in Charts 2015," November 2015, http://publications.apec.org/publication-detail.php?pub_id=1675.

2. ADB, *Asia 2050: Realizing the Asian Century: Executive Summary* (Manila: ADB, August 2011), https://www.adb.org/publications/asia-2050-realizing-asian-century.

It is useful to consider a few of the more specific elements of the ADB's "Asian Century" scenario. By 2050, China will have seen its GDP per capita triple from $14,000 to almost $50,000. India will experience a similarly massive transformation, reaching an average income level equivalent to that of France or the United Kingdom today. Indonesia, the world's third-largest democracy by population, will rise from its current place as a top-20 global economy to a true heavyweight in the top five of the global GDP tables. Many of Asia's other developing economies—Vietnam, Bangladesh, the Philippines, Pakistan, and Malaysia—will be among the fastest growing in the world.[3] Meanwhile, the wealthy and developed economies of Asia today—Japan, South Korea, Taiwan, and Singapore—will grow at a slower pace but remain key leaders in technology and innovation.

The United States has benefited enormously from its economic involvement in a growing Asia-Pacific region. In 2015, U.S. goods and services exports to Asia were more than $750 billion, a figure that has roughly doubled over the past decade.[4] These exports support more than 3 million jobs across the United States;[5] 39 states send a quarter or more of their exports to Asia.[6] The region is also a key source of inbound foreign direct investment (FDI). As of year-end 2015, Asian companies had invested more than $564 billion in the U.S. economy—still only one-quarter the stock of European investment but growing at a faster pace.[7] These investments, too, have significant employment benefits: investments from Asia in the automobile sector alone directly or indirectly support more than 1.5 million jobs in the United States.[8] Moreover, jobs with Asian and other foreign-affiliated firms operating in the United States often pay well above the U.S. average.[9] As a region, Asia accounts for around half of all foreign holdings of U.S. government securities and significant volumes of inbound portfolio investment.[10]

U.S. engagement with Asia through imports and outbound investment is no less critical. In 2015, the United States imported nearly $1.3 trillion worth of goods and services from Asia and Pacific

---

3. PricewaterhouseCoopers (PWC), *The World in 2050: Will the Shift in Global Economic Power Continue?* (London: PWC, 2015), https://www.pwc.com/gx/en/issues/the-economy/assets/world-in-2050-february-2015.pdf.

4. Bureau of Economic Analysis (BEA), "International Transactions, Table 1.3. U.S. International Transactions, Expanded Details by Area and Country," U.S. Department of Commerce, accessed October 2016, http://www.bea.gov/iTable/index_ita.cfm.

5. Chris Rasmussen and Susan Xu, "Jobs Supported by Export Destination 2015," Office of Trade and Economic Analysis, September 2016, http://www.trade.gov/mas/ian/build/groups/public/@tg_ian/documents/webcontent/tg_ian_005508.pdf.

6. Asia Matters for America, "Asia Matters for America Highlights," East-West Center, accessed October 2016, http://www.asiamattersforamerica.org/overview.

7. BEA, "Direct Investment and Multinational Enterprises, Foreign Direct Investment Position in the United States on a Historical-Cost Basis," U.S. Department of Commerce, accessed October 2016, http://www.bea.gov/iTable/index_MNC.cfm.

8. Thomas J. Prusa, *The Contribution of the Japanese-Brand Automotive Industry to the United States Economy* (Washington, DC: Japan Automobile Manufacturers Association, July 2016), http://www.jama.org/the-contribution-of-the-japanese-branded-automotive-industry-to-the-united-states-economy-2015-update/.

9. Theodore H. Moran and Lindsay Oldenski, "Japanese Investment in the United States: Superior Performance, Increasing Integration," Policy Brief, Peterson Institute for International Economics, February 2015, https://piie.com/publications/pb/pb15-3.pdf.

10. U.S. Department of the Treasury, "Major Foreign Holders of Treasury Securities," September 16, 2016, http://ticdata.treasury.gov/Publish/mfh.txt.

economies, more than any other region. On a historical-cost basis, U.S. companies had invested $778 billion in Asian economies as of end-2015.[11] These investments by American firms have helped to integrate Asia into extensive global supply chains and driven a large share of trans-Pacific trade. For example, China is the world's single-largest market for finished semiconductors, accounting for nearly 30 percent of global demand.[12] These chips help to power more $500 billion in Chinese exports, but the chips themselves—and most of the value and intellectual property represented in these exports—are both produced in the United States as well as by U.S. companies invested in Asia.[13]

China has been a major driver of U.S. involvement in Asia. For almost four decades, China enjoyed average annual growth rates above 9 percent, driving a more than 25-fold increase in its GDP from 1978 to 2015. This tremendous expansion lifted more than 600 million Chinese out of poverty,[14] and helped to supercharge growth throughout the region, especially in Southeast Asia. Though not without problems, discussed below, China's growth also created benefits for the United States, helping to keep costs down for American consumers and generating new export opportunities for U.S. companies and workers. From 2000 to 2015, U.S. exports to China grew an average of almost 13 percent annually, more than twice as fast as U.S. exports to the rest of the world. Given that per capita GDP in China is still barely a quarter that of the United States, there is enormous room for further growth. This will have to come at a slower pace in order to be sustainable, but as China transitions toward a more consumption-led, innovation-based growth model (and expands its international investment footprint), the opportunities for strengthening the U.S.-China economic relationship may be even greater.[15]

Southeast Asia and India also represent bright spots for growth and opportunities for American firms and workers. The 10 members of ASEAN had a combined economy of $2.5 trillion in 2015; considered as a bloc they are the third-largest economy in Asia after China and Japan, ahead of India, and seventh largest in the world.[16] Collectively, ASEAN has been the second-fastest-growing economy in Asia after China over the past decade.[17] With a population of 630 million and demographics that skew young, ASEAN is poised to continue growing at high rates. The stock of U.S. direct investment in ASEAN totaled $250 billion at the end of 2015, more than all U.S. investment

11. BEA, "Direct Investment and Multinational Enterprises."

12. U.S. International Trade Administration (ITA), "2016 ITA Semiconductors and Semiconductor Manufacturing Equipment Top Markets Report," July 2016, http://trade.gov/topmarkets/pdf/Semiconductors_China.pdf.

13. Gordon Orr and Christopher Thomas, "Semiconductors in China: Brave New World or Same Old Story?," McKinsey & Company, August 2014, http://www.mckinsey.com/industries/high-tech/our-insights/semiconductors-in-china-brave-new-world-or-same-old-story.

14. World Bank, "Results Profile: China Poverty Reduction," March 19, 2010, http://www.worldbank.org/en/news/feature/2010/03/19/results-profile-china-poverty-reduction.

15. Wojciech Maliszewski et al., "Resolving China's Corporate Debt Problem," October 14 2016, International Monetary Fund, https://www.imf.org/external/pubs/cat/longres.aspx?sk=44337.0.

16. IMF, *World Economic Outlook: Too Slow for Too Long* (Washington, DC: IMF, April 2016), http://www.imf.org/external/pubs/ft/weo/2016/01/.

17. Ibid.

in China, India, South Korea, Hong Kong, Taiwan, and New Zealand combined.[18] Within ASEAN, Vietnam is the rising star, with GDP growth projected to average 6.3 percent annually from 2015 to 2021,[19] and with economic policies and favorable demographics that are attracting large flows of inward foreign direct investment—projected to reach $15 billion in 2016.[20] The Philippines is another country enjoying relatively high rates of economic growth, with a growing middle class, although the more belligerent stance of the current president, Rodrigo Duterte, is cause for significant concern.

Meanwhile, India has been posting annual growth rates above 7 percent for the past two years, and the International Monetary Fund (IMF) projects that this growth will accelerate over the next five.[21] Should New Delhi stay committed to responsible macroeconomic management and succeed in implementing even modest structural reforms, India's growth could surprise on the upside of this forecast. Moreover, given the current low level of per capita income—less than half that of China, on a purchasing power parity basis—it is possible that India could sustain this rapid growth rate for an extended period of time. Over the long term, estimates indicate that what is today a $2.3 trillion economy could become the world's second largest by 2050.[22]

In addition to this country-specific potential, two sectors offer particular promise for U.S. exporters to Asia:

- *Services:* American services providers are leaders in sectors from health care and transport to information security and finance. In 2015, Asia accounted for less than 30 percent of U.S. services exports, but this figure is poised to grow significantly due to major economic and demographic transitions under way in the region.[23] With increased wealth, Asian tourists are traveling and spending money abroad at an unprecedented pace; the United States is well positioned to compete for a large share of this business.[24] Over the next 20 years, the number of individuals in Asia aged 65 and older will grow more than 20 percent per annum, creating new opportunities for American health care and insurance providers.[25] As Internet penetration rates rise and Asian governments and companies make greater use of digital

18. Asia Matters for America, "U.S.-ASEAN Investments," East-West Center, accessed October 2016, http://www.asiamattersforamerica.org/asean/data/trade/investments.

19. IMF, *World Economic Outlook: Too Slow for Too Long.*

20. My Pham, "Vietnam's Jan-Sept FDI Inflow to Rise 12.4 pct y/y to $11.02 bln—Govt," Reuters, September 23, 2016, http://www.reuters.com/article/vietnam-economy-fdi-idUSL3N1BY2UR.

21. IMF, "World Economic Outlook Database," accessed October 2016, https://www.imf.org/external/pubs/ft/weo/2016/02/weodata/index.aspx

22. ADB, *Asia 2050: Realizing the Asian Century: Executive Summary.*

23. Independent estimates have shown that TPP would also enhance these opportunities. See Peter A. Petri and Michael G. Plummer, "The Economic Effects of the Trans-Pacific Partnership: New Estimates" (working paper, Peterson Institute for International Economics, January 2016), https://piie.com/system/files/documents/wp16-2_0.pdf.

24. UN World Tourism Organization (UNWTO), *UNTWO Tourism Highlights: 2015 Edition* (Madrid: UNTWO, 2015), http://www.e-unwto.org/doi/pdf/10.18111/9789284416899.

25. World Bank, "Rapid Aging in East Asia and Pacific Will Shrink Workforce and Increase Public Spending," December 9, 2015, http://www.worldbank.org/en/region/eap/brief/rapid-aging-in-east-asia-and-pacific-will-shrink-workforce-increase-public-spending.

technologies, the demand for Internet-related technology, e-commerce, big-data analyties, and cybersecurity services will increase significantly. The overall process of development will also generate increased demand for U.S. intellectual property, potentially leading to significant increases in revenues from software sales, trademarks, and other services.

- *Energy:* The U.S. Energy Information Agency (EIA) projects that world energy consumption will grow nearly 50 percent over the next quarter century. Demand from Asia accounts for more than half of this expected increase, led by growth in China and India.[26] Again, the United States is well positioned to take advantage of these trends. In 2015, total U.S. energy production increased for the sixth consecutive year, while annual net imports fell for the 10th year in a row.[27] Aided by recent infrastructure developments, such as the opening of a natural gas liquefaction plant in the Gulf of Mexico, U.S. natural gas exports are becoming more competitive in Asia and are already beginning to travel across the Pacific.[28] For energy-poor allies, such as Japan and South Korea, the addition of a reliable new source of energy has strategic as well as economic benefits, providing an opportunity to deepen cooperation with the United States. Renewable energy and energy-efficient technologies provide further opportunities for U.S. businesses as Asia's aggregate demand grows. From high-performance natural gas turbines to green transport and advanced grid management and energy storage, U.S. technological leadership combined with Asia's energy needs represents a clear opportunity for mutually beneficial exchange.

ECONOMIC CHALLENGES RISING

Despite the promise of the Asia Pacific, the region faces significant obstacles. China and other emerging countries are facing the "middle-income trap," in which the benefits of cheap labor dwindle before a country is competitive in higher-value-added production. Ensuring that growth is inclusive—providing benefits across internal and external boundaries, ethnic and social groups, and income levels—remains a significant economic and political challenge across the region. Investing in patterns of urbanization that are both growth enhancing and environmentally sustainable will be vital. Improvements in institutional quality and governance—areas where Asia has traditionally lagged—are also critical to success.

In the near term, the Asia Pacific has a growth problem. Nearly a decade after the global financial crisis, the region's advanced economies are still struggling to find their footing. Annual growth in each of the region's five largest advanced economies—the United States, Japan, South Korea, Australia, and Taiwan—has averaged below 3 percent over the past five years.[29] In emerging and

26. U.S. Energy Information Administration (EIA), *International Energy Outlook 2016* (Washington, DC: EIA, May 2016), http://www.eia.gov/forecasts/ieo/.

27. EIA, "Total U.S. Energy Production Increases for Sixth Consecutive Year," April 18, 2016, http://www.eia.gov/todayinenergy/detail.cfm?id=25852.

28. Harry Weber and Naureen Malik, "America's Shale Gas Heads to East Asia for First Time," Bloomberg, July 27, 2016, http://www.bloomberg.com/news/articles/2016-07-27/america-s-shale-gas-is-heading-to-the-far-east-for-first-time.

29. IMF, "World Economic Outlook Database."

developing Asia, growth has averaged 7.4 percent—high in absolute terms but nearly a full percentage point lower than the precrisis trend. The slowdown in growth has been especially pronounced in China, where annual growth rates have reached their lowest levels in a quarter century and may be even lower than official statistics suggest. Beijing has acknowledged the need to shift from the investment- and export-led growth model of the past toward a more innovation- and consumption-led model. However, rising aggregate debt levels, moribund economic reform, the resurgence of inefficient or monopolistic state-owned enterprises, and repeated policy missteps or reversals suggest that Chinese leaders are struggling to manage the economic challenges they face.

As the days of double-digit Chinese growth recede, it is clear that no other country has the size and momentum to drive regional growth. Despite India's emergence as the fastest-growing major Asian economy in recent years, its limited economic heft and relatively weak linkages to the region limit the extent to which this growth exerts positive momentum. India's nominal GDP is roughly $2 trillion, less than half that of Japan, and GDP per capita—a measure that overstates the purchasing power of the average Indian consumer—is less than half that of China. Fewer than half of India's top-20 trading partners are in South and East Asia.[30] This is due in part to India's continued unwillingness to dismantle barriers to trade and investment.

Moreover, there are significant risks looming over Asia's growth prospects. Recent growth has only been achieved through significant increases in debt in both advanced and developing economies. From 2007 to 2014, six Asian economies—Singapore, China, Japan, Malaysia, South Korea, and Thailand—saw their aggregate debt-to-GDP ratios increase by more than 40 percent.[31] Elevated rates of debt accumulation and declining efficiency of credit utilization are typically associated with increased vulnerability to financial crisis.[32] Moreover, Asia has seen subdued levels of fixed asset investment by business, reflecting cautious private-sector sentiment. This has a negative impact on near-term growth and could reduce potential growth over the medium term.[33]

Meanwhile, large developing economies in the region, such as India, Indonesia, and the Philippines, are struggling to manage the rapid pace of urbanization and the need to employ their large and young populations. For these countries, below-potential growth rates could have serious social and political consequences; if policymakers are unable to meet growing demand for quality urban jobs, they could see their countries' demographic dividends erode significantly.

The countries of Northeast Asia face the opposite challenge. Japan, South Korea, and China are all rapidly aging economies with shrinking workforces and rising health and retirement needs. As this

---

30. Indian Ministry of Commerce and Industry, "Export Import Data Bank Version 7.1," April 2016, http://commerce.nic.in/eidb/default.asp.

31. Richard Dobbs, Susan Lund, Jonathan Woetzel, and Mina Mutafchieva, *Debt and (Not Much) Deleveraging*, McKinsey Global Institute, February 2015, http://www.mckinsey.com/global-themes/employment-and-growth/debt-and-not-much-deleveraging.

32. Stijn Claessens and M. Ayhan Kose, *Financial Crises: Explanations, Types, and Implications*, IMF Working Paper (Washington, DC: IMF, January 2013), https://www.imf.org/external/pubs/ft/wp/2013/wp1328.pdf.

33. IMF, *World Economic Outlook: Uneven Growth: Short- and Long-Term Factors* (Washington, DC: IMF, April 2015), https://www.imf.org/external/pubs/ft/weo/2015/01/pdf/c4.pdf.

demographic process continues, welfare spending is expected to consume an increasing share of public expenditures and the number of workers-per-beneficiary will decline. If not balanced by consistent productivity increases, efficient investment, GDP growth, and corresponding increases in fiscal revenue, the result will be a sharp deterioration of public finances.

In theory, each of these problems is the solution to the other. India, Indonesia, the Philippines, and Bangladesh each has a population over 100 million that is still growing rapidly. Deepening pools of labor in South and Southeast Asia can help to balance shrinking workforces in the economies of Northeast Asia, home to the oldest and fastest-aging countries in the world (Japan and South Korea, respectively). Meanwhile, surplus capital in Northeast Asia could be deployed to meet the need for fixed asset investment in peninsular Southeast Asia and the countries surrounding the Bay of Bengal.

However, other impediments get in the way of these flows. Relative to their level of development, Asian countries continue to underperform the rest of the world on major governance indicators: control of corruption; rule of law; regulatory quality; government effectiveness; voice and accountability; and political stability.[34] This poor performance helps to explain a number of issues, including the region's enormous infrastructure spending deficit, estimated by the ADB to be on the order of $800 billion annually.[35] It is difficult to attract long-term investment flows without legal and institutional structures that are transparent, strong, and stable.

Meanwhile, protectionist, mercantilist, and nationalist forces are on the rise in the Asia Pacific.[36] Under the "Make in India" initiative, the administration of Narendra Modi appears determined to pursue a discredited import-substitution development model. In Jakarta, the government of Joko Widodo (Jokowi) continues to flirt with economic nationalism and a range of protectionist policies. China is pursuing mercantilist trade and investment policies across numerous economic sectors, including subsidized, standards-fueled, exclusionary technology policies, such as its "Made in China 2025" plan and national security law.[37] If left unchecked, these restrictions could undermine regional growth and integration, as well as lead to greater political tension.

Another major set of challenges for Asia is growing resource scarcity and environmental degradation. The demographic shifts and rising incomes across Asia (described previously) have placed increased burdens on natural resources. Worldwide demand for food, water, and energy is expected to grow by 35, 40, and 50 percent, respectively, from the present through 2030, largely driven by Asia's growth.[38] Even with continued improvements in the efficiency of resource

34. Harinder S. Kohli, Ashok Sharma, and Anil Sood, *Asia 2050: Realizing the Asian Century* (New York: ADB/Sage Publications, 2011), https://www.adb.org/publications/asia-2050-realizing-asian-century.

35. ADB, *Infrastructure for a Seamless Asia* (Manila: ADB, 2009), https://www.adb.org/sites/default/files/publication/159348/adbi-infrastructure-seamless-asia.pdf.

36. Simon J Evenett and Johannes Fritz, *The Tide Turns? Trade, Protectionism, and Slowing Global Growth: The 18th Global Trade Alert Report* (London: CEPR Press, 2015), http://www.globaltradealert.org/sites/default/files/GTA18%20The%20Tide%20Turns.pdf.

37. Scott Kennedy and Christopher K. Johnson, *Perfecting China, Inc.: The 13th Five-Year Plan* (Washington, DC: CSIS, May 2016), https://csis-prod.s3.amazonaws.com/s3fs-public/publication/160521_Kennedy_PerfectingChinaInc_Web.pdf.

38. National Intelligence Council, *Global Trends 2030: Alternative Worlds* (Washington, DC: National Intelligence Council, November 2012), https://globaltrends2030.files.wordpress.com/2012/11/global-trends-2030-november2012.pdf.

allocation and use, physical constraints are emerging. Over 20 percent of arable land worldwide is degraded.[39] This figure is far worse in some Asian countries, including China and India. Water stress is expected to increase across virtually all of Asia in the coming decades, most notably in China, India, and Vietnam.[40] According to World Health Organization (WHO) data on urban air quality, Asia is home to 37 of the world's most polluted cities, with India and China together accounting for 60 percent of the leaderboard.[41] Resource scarcity and environmental degradation are looming threats to Asia's long-term economic growth and the health of the region's population, raising the risk of instability or conflict.[42]

REGIONAL SECURITY TRENDS

These challenges are exacerbated by shifts in the security environment in the Asia Pacific, which have implications for U.S. economic and strategic involvement in the region. The post–World War II, U.S.-led security architecture remains the lynchpin of stability in the Asia Pacific. Relations with key allies, especially Japan, South Korea, and Australia, are strong and have grown stronger in recent years. Long-standing ties with partners such as Singapore continue to provide anchors for U.S. engagement, and there are growing opportunities for enhanced relations with new friends and emerging partners, such as Vietnam and India.

However, the regional security landscape is evolving. Far from diminishing, the threat posed by North Korea's development of nuclear weapons capability has intensified. Under the administration of Xi Jinping, China is investing in military modernization, being more assertive in the region, and showing a new willingness to undermine regional norms and flout international law, most notably in the South China Sea. These challenges persist alongside nontraditional security threats, such as terrorism, cyber-attacks, pandemics, and environmental disasters (including extreme weather events).

The shifting security climate has generated a renewed demand for active U.S. involvement in the region. In particular, China's assertiveness in maritime spaces has led many Asian countries (including former U.S. adversaries) to seek closer security relations with the United States. Yet these countries also want deeper U.S. participation in the region's economic affairs as another vital underpinning of stability. Against this background, the rhetoric of the 2016 presidential campaign

---

39. Lutz Goedde, Maya Horii, and Sunil Sanghvi, "Pursuing the Global Opportunity in Food and Agribusiness," McKinsey & Company, July 2015, http://www.mckinsey.com/insights/food_agriculture/pursuing_the_global_opportunity_in_food_and_agribusiness.

40. Office of the Director of National Intelligence, "Global Water: Present to 2025," February 2012, http://www.dni.gov/files/documents/Special%20Report_Global%20Water%20Security%20Map.pdf.

41. World Health Organization (WHO), "WHO Global Urban Ambient Air Pollution Database (update 2016)," http://www.who.int/phe/health_topics/outdoorair/databases/cities/en/.

42. Alex Evans, *Resource Scarcity, Climate Change, and the Risk of Violent Conflict*, World Development Report 2011 Background Paper (Washington, DC: World Bank, September 2010), http://web.worldbank.org/archive/website01306/web/pdf/wdr%20background%20paper_evans_04dbd.pdf?keepThis=true&TB_iframe=true&height=600&width=800.

and the failure to ratify TPP have raised concerns in Asia about U.S. commitment to the region and the sustainability of the vital balancing role played by the United States.

But calls for closer U.S. ties by Asian countries are accompanied by their desire for productive relations with China as well. Most countries in Asia are anxious to avoid a "choice" between Washington and Beijing, particularly in light of their growing economic interdependence with China. Thus Washington policymakers will need to strike a careful balance in exerting confident leadership without excluding or diminishing China's legitimate role.

REGIONAL ECONOMIC ARCHITECTURE

Regional institution building has been a central feature of Asia-Pacific affairs over the past several decades. An alphabet soup of political and economic arrangements, from ASEAN to APEC to the EAS, has emerged. Many of these arrangements are "soft" in the sense that they do not involve deep pooling of sovereignty or legally binding commitments. Nevertheless, the impulse to gather regional political leaders and officials in search of consensus and common interest is strong.

ASEAN, founded in the late 1960s as a bulwark against communism in the region, has taken on an increasingly central role in these developments. Following the Asian financial crisis, large powers in the region such as Japan and China sought to deepen ties with the Southeast Asian grouping via a series of "ASEAN-plus" initiatives: ASEAN+1 trade agreements and ASEAN+3 (China, Japan, Korea) financial arrangements such as the Chiang Mai Initiative, which is a network of central bank swap facilities. ASEAN was also the driver behind the launch of the EAS in 2005, initially an ASEAN+6 (China, Japan, Korea, Australia, New Zealand, and India) arrangement but joined by the United States and Russia in 2011. Meanwhile, ASEAN moved to deepen its own internal economic integration with the formal debut in late 2015 of the ASEAN Economic Community (AEC).

ASEAN has also been at the heart of a proliferation of trade arrangements in the Asia Pacific over the past 15 years. In 2000, the number of active free-trade agreements (FTAs) involving Asian countries was 35; as of mid-2016, that number had risen to 140, with 75 either under negotiation or signed but not yet in effect.[43] ASEAN itself has signed FTAs with six regional partners, and negotiations are under way for a Regional Comprehensive Economic Partnership (RCEP) that will link ASEAN and these six trading partners in a regional trade arrangement.

While not a member of all of the ASEAN and regional arrangements, the United States has an important stake in institution building in the Asia Pacific, both in the economic and security arenas. Washington's participation in building an effective regional architecture is seen as a natural extension of its invaluable contribution to regional peace and prosperity over decades. U.S. leadership helps set the agenda and makes institutions more effective and responsive. Time thus spent reinforces the American strategic position in Asia, as well as promoting rules, norms, and practices that benefit U.S. economic and security interests.

43. Asia Regional Integration Center, "Free Trade Agreements," accessed October 2016, https://aric.adb.org/fta-all.

Since 1989, the Asia Pacific Economic Cooperation (APEC) forum has been the principal vehicle for Washington's involvement in regional economic institution building. APEC brings together 21 Pacific Rim economies to advance trade and investment liberalization through a nonbinding, consensus-based process. Though sprawling and often amorphous, APEC has regained momentum in recent years and made some valuable contributions to regional (and global) economic integration. For example, in its host year in 2011, Washington brokered a landmark agreement among APEC leaders to commit to environmental goods liberalization, which has since driven progress toward a binding agreement at the multilateral level. APEC spearheaded the original Information Technology Agreement (ITA) in 1996 and played a leading role in updating the agreement in 2015 (ITA-2).[44]

Over the past several years, however, the regional trade agenda has been driven by TPP, which has been the centerpiece of U.S. economic policy in the Asia Pacific. Linking 12 Pacific Rim economies representing some 40 percent of global GDP, TPP is designed to substantially liberalize market access across the group and establish high-standard rules that support twenty-first-century trade and investment.[45]

TPP advances U.S. interests by expanding American export and job opportunities; by creating new and updated rules in areas critical to today's globalized economy, such as services, digital trade, and state-owned enterprises; and by complementing our military strategy in Asia.

Having been concluded in the fall of 2015 and signed in early 2016, the TPP agreement now requires approval in the legislatures of the 12 member countries before entry into force. Ratification by the U.S. Congress, once considered likely, has now been indefinitely delayed. But the fact remains that implementation of a high-standard TPP agreement is vital not only to U.S. economic interests but also to U.S. security, credibility, and success in the Asia Pacific.

Meanwhile, other institutional developments not involving the United States are moving ahead across the region. RCEP, a trade negotiation among the ASEAN+6 countries, represents a low-standard alternative to TPP that has been gaining momentum in recent months and is now on a path toward conclusion. In finance, China, dissatisfied with the pace of reform in governance of existing institutions such as the World Bank and the IMF, has been active in creating new institutions. Most prominent among these is the AIIB, a Beijing-based alternative to the ADB established in 2015. China has also announced its own ambitious initiative to finance infrastructure investment across the Asia Pacific, dubbed "One Belt, One Road" (OBOR).[46] Other new Chinese-led institutional arrangements include alternative international payment systems and credit-rating services.[47]

---

44. APEC, "Market Access Group," accessed October 2016, http://www.apec.org/Groups/Committee-on-Trade-and-Investment/Market-Access-Group.aspx.

45. Office of the U.S. Trade Representative, "Trans-Pacific Partnership," accessed October 2016, https://ustr.gov/tpp/.

46. Christopher K. Johnson, *President Xi Jinping's "Belt and Road" Initiative: A Practical Assessment of the Chinese Communist Party's Roadmap for China's Global Resurgence* (Washington, DC: CSIS, March 2016), https://csis-prod.s3.amazonaws.com/s3fs-public/publication/160328_Johnson_PresidentXiJinping_Web.pdf.

47. Sebastian Hellmann, Moritz Rudolf, Mikko Huotari, and Johannes Buckow, "China's Shadow Foreign Policy: Parallel Structures Challenge the Established International Order," *MERICS China Monitor*, no. 18 (October 28, 2014), http://www.merics.org/fileadmin/templates/download/china-monitor/China_Monitor_No_18_en.pdf.

Regional institution building in the Asia Pacific is inherently messy; for the foreseeable future, no single architecture is likely to prevail in a region so diverse, with competing bids for leadership. A certain amount of competition over the most appropriate institutions, rules, and norms for the region can be healthy; that China is now championing the Free Trade Area of the Asia Pacific (FTAAP), originally a U.S. initiative, illustrates this. But the United States has an interest in remaining a highly active participant in Asia-Pacific institution building to ensure continued progress toward an open, rules-based, trans-Pacific order that improves economic and security outcomes for the United States and the entire region.

03

Keys to a Successful U.S. Strategy

Against a shifting Asia-Pacific landscape, the incoming U.S. administration will need an effective strategy that continues to support and extend U.S. interests in the region. The strategy will need to be comprehensive, covering economic, security, and diplomatic engagement. It will need to be put in place early and carried out with constancy and effectiveness, with coordinated contributions from across the U.S. government. And it will need to be persuasive both to the American public and to those in Asia.

Economics must be at the heart of any successful strategy in Asia, for four reasons. First, as described in Chapter 2, no region of the world offers more economic and commercial opportunities for American businesses and workers. Second, economic integration is viewed in the Asia Pacific as strategic in nature, a critical underpinning of peace and stability. Third, most Asian countries want the United States deeply involved in the region's economic affairs as a complement to our military presence and to limit their overdependence on China. And finally, the United States has a major stake in ensuring that the economic rules in the Asia Pacific continue to support U.S. interests.

U.S. economic and security interests require a stable, predictable order in the Asia Pacific, supported by transparent institutions and rules. As a Pacific but not an Asian power, the United States should ensure that this order is not exclusive to Asia but rather trans-Pacific, incorporating countries on the eastern rim of the Pacific Ocean. And of course the United States has a broader interest in peace and stability in the region, free from coercive or destabilizing behavior; this both supports and is supported by our economic interests.

In formulating its strategy, the new administration does not need to reinvent the wheel. The last eight presidents, from Richard Nixon through Barack Obama, have laid down a sound framework for strategic involvement in the Asia Pacific. This includes working to pull China, Vietnam, and other formerly isolated countries more deeply into the rules-based order; pressing for open markets, transparency, and rule of law across the region; promoting growth-enhancing policies and building capacity in developing countries; and participating actively in regional institution building. The key for the new administration will be to strengthen and focus these efforts while carrying them out vigorously and consistently.

What follows in this chapter and the next is not a detailed blueprint for a strategy to be pursued by the incoming administration. Events and policy preferences will vary; flexibility should be maintained. Rather, we suggest a set of broad goals that are consistent with enduring U.S. interests in the Asia Pacific and that can usefully guide the next administration's approach to Asian economic strategy. This is followed in Chapter 4 by eight high-level policy recommendations and a series of specific implementation steps under each.

STRATEGIC OBJECTIVES

Four broad strategic goals should guide U.S. economic policy in the Asia Pacific over the next administration:

- *Promoting strong, sustainable, balanced, and inclusive growth*: Growth is a principal objective of all economic policy. It brings jobs, rising incomes, and fiscal resources. The Asia Pacific has been and is likely to remain the fastest-growing region of the world, and it is vital to U.S. interests that we benefit from this growth.

  At the Pittsburgh Summit in September 2009, leaders of the Group of 20 (G20) economies agreed to a framework of policy coordination to achieve "strong, sustainable, and balanced global growth." With the addition of the adjective "inclusive" at the 2016 Hangzhou Summit, this phrase has been the organizing principle of the G20. Half the members of the G20 are the Asia-Pacific economies, so it would be natural to reinforce this goal by making it a central theme in U.S. economic policy toward the region.

  At a time of uneven and uncertain growth across the region, all Asia-Pacific economies should be encouraged to use an appropriate mix of monetary, fiscal, and structural policies to raise demand and remove supply-side constraints to growth. All regional economies could benefit from more investment in infrastructure and policies to make growth more inclusive—that is, providing more opportunities for small and medium-sized enterprises (SMEs), women, and youth. All economies could be made more efficient and competitive by opening their markets further and pursuing regulatory reform. Governance and rule of law in many countries need to be strengthened.

  Policy priorities vary for different sub-groups of Asia-Pacific economies. In the advanced and large emerging countries, the emphasis should be on rebalancing growth toward domestic demand. China is a case in point. As its leadership recognizes, the old model of investment- and export-led growth is unsustainable; growth needs to be driven more by domestic consumption and services. Similarly, Japan, Korea, and Taiwan need to do more to stimulate domestic demand.

  For Asian economies such as India, Indonesia, and the Philippines, the priority should be on opening markets to trade and investment, improving regulation and regulatory transparency, and strengthening the rule of law. The United States can encourage these reforms by maintaining its open markets but also insisting on appropriate policy adjustments, including with regard to the treatment of U.S. exports and investment in those countries.

- *Improving the competitive landscape for U.S. companies*: During the past few decades of rapid growth, Asia has emerged as a vital export market and production base for U.S. companies. The continued rapid expansion and integration of the region's economies and middle class will reinforce these trends.

  Especially in industries where economies of scale and network effects are essential to competitiveness, active involvement in Asia will be critical to ensuring a robust and successful U.S. private sector.[1] This is particularly true for sectors such as high technology and advanced manufacturing, where the United States has clear comparative advantages.

  A competitive landscape for U.S. companies—multinationals and SMEs alike—requires more than reducing tariffs and other border barriers to trade. Because U.S. companies are often leaders in their sectors and invest heavily in research and development, they are uniquely vulnerable to intellectual property (IP) theft, technology expropriation or forced technology transfer, cyber-attacks, and economic espionage. Robust IP regimes, rule of law, and regulatory transparency in the markets in which they operate are essential to the competitiveness of U.S. firms. These are areas of persistent weakness in Asia. As a result, a major focus of Washington's economic strategy must be on encouraging countries to engage in a "race to the top" and responding to countries that undermine these principles.

  The success of American businesses in Asia does more than narrowly benefit the U.S. economy. By investing in local facilities and training local workforces, U.S. firms support rising incomes for Asian workers and new markets for high-quality American products. Through adherence to high standards on issues such as labor rights and honest practices, U.S. companies act as ambassadors for American culture and values. By pushing to remove barriers to U.S. exports and investment, such as restrictions on foreign ownership, and working to ensure a level playing field for U.S. businesses, Washington can also help partner economies in their efforts to overcome vested interests and achieve growth-enhancing structural reform.

- *Advancing trans-Pacific regional economic integration*: The Asia Pacific is in the midst of a decades-long but fitful march toward greater regional economic integration. The United States has a strong stake in trans-Pacific forms of integration and should continue to be active in promoting them. This includes continuing to work closely with Canada and key Pacific-facing Latin American partners like Mexico, Peru, and Chile. The United States also has an interest in fostering an open, rules-based economic order in the region. In addition to

---

1. For example, the Asia Pacific accounted for almost 60 percent of global semiconductor sales in 2013 and a similar share of global industrial robotics sales in 2014. See Semiconductor Industry Association, "The U.S. Semiconductor Industry: 2014 Factbook," 2014, http://www.semiconductors.org/clientuploads/Industry%20Statistics/2014%20Factbook%202.0%20-%2002032015.pdf; and International Federation of Robotics (IFR), *World Robotics: Industrial Robots, 2015* (Frankfurt am Main: IFR, 2015), http://www.ifr.org/industrial-robots/statistics/.

ensuring a level playing field for American companies, integration along these lines will boost regional growth and promote regional stability.

Working with allies and partners in the region should be central to U.S. efforts to promote regional economic integration. Countries such as Japan, Australia, South Korea, and Singapore have demonstrated a willingness and ability to help promote a regional order based on high-standard rules and norms. This can be seen in the long-standing cooperation the United States has enjoyed from these partners in APEC and more recently TPP.

The United States could do more to encourage ASEAN economic integration. A more open and prosperous ASEAN is good for American trade and investment, and a more unified and resilient ASEAN would bring strategic benefits to the United States and the region. To date, ASEAN's own efforts to integrate its 10 member economies into a single market and production base have been slow and halting. The ASEAN Economic Community was launched with much fanfare in December 2015, yet despite some real progress in lowering trade barriers, nontariff barriers have actually risen over the past decade and continue to impede cross-border trade within ASEAN. National regulations affecting trade and investment are far from harmonized at the regional level.[2] U.S. support for ASEAN economic integration efforts, such as assistance for the ASEAN Single Window to facilitate trade, would be helpful. But more ambitious steps, such as a U.S.-ASEAN free-trade agreement, will have to wait until ASEAN can take more decisive steps to remove structural barriers to trade within the group.

- *Enhancing cooperation on transnational challenges*: Asia is prone to a range of problems that cross national borders, from health pandemics to earthquakes. The region's borders are porous and sometimes ill defined. Many of Asia's largest urban areas are coastal and exposed to both natural disasters and the threat of climate change. Disease outbreaks are difficult to monitor and prevent and can spread easily. Thus there is a premium on coordination and cooperation in Asia to mitigate and address these risks.

The United States is well positioned to assist. The armed forces and U.S. Agency for International Development (USAID) have unique capabilities and experience in providing humanitarian assistance and disaster response in the region. Through the Centers for Disease Control and other U.S. government entities, the United States provides unequaled leadership in responding to global health challenges. Bringing American resources to bear in this way can help to prevent the spread of damaging crises, support economic growth and stability, and generate goodwill in the region.

The U.S. private sector has an important role to play in this regard. Financial services firms, including insurance companies, can provide resources that allow disaster-hit areas to quickly recover. U.S. companies are leaders in energy-efficient technologies, health care delivery, and climate-resilient infrastructure. They can also help make Asian economies more resilient by addressing the needs of Asia's aging populations through better long-term

2. Lili Yan Ing, Santiago Fernandez de Cordoba, and Olivier Cadot, eds., *Non-Tariff Measures in ASEAN* (Geneva: UN Conference on Trade and Development, April 2016), http://unctad.org/en/PublicationsLibrary/ERIA-UNCTAD_Non-Tariff_Measures_in_ASEAN_en.pdf.

health care and retirement solutions. Each of these areas represents economic opportunity for U.S. and Asian firms and is an essential complement to prevention and recovery.

GUIDING PRINCIPLES

Establishing broad strategic objectives to guide policymaking is a critical element of an effective strategy. Implementation is also vital. Much of the effectiveness of U.S. strategy in Asia will hinge on the successful promotion of a whole-of-government mindset and strong but flexible policymaking processes. Busy policymakers can all too easily be overtaken by external events or become captive to the demands of a single initiative or bilateral relationship rather than informed by a consistent strategic perspective.

We offer below a set of five guiding principles for policymakers in the next administration. We envisage these as a checklist that every senior policymaker should review before any meeting or discussion—in the interagency process, with foreign counterparts, or with outside stakeholders:

- *Begin and end with U.S. interests*: As discussed already, the United States has an enduring set of strategic interests in the Asia Pacific: open markets; a trans-Pacific, rules-based order; peace and stability. To be successful and to earn the support of Congress and the American people, the next administration's economic strategy toward Asia must protect and promote these interests.
- *Use incentives and disincentives strategically*: Good international economic policy is about the strategic use of positive and negative incentives, or "carrots and sticks." As it did in TPP, the United States can use the offer of preferential access to the world's largest consumer market and our capital as a means of encouraging market opening and reform in Asian economies. But it should also be willing to use targeted tools available under U.S. and international law (and to consider new tools) to address unfair treatment of U.S. companies and workers—for example, insisting on greater reciprocity in trade and investment.
- *Mobilize and support the private sector*: A core strength of the United States is its private sector. American companies have enormous technical capabilities, know-how, capital, and experience in trading and investing in Asia. Engaging with and supporting the private sector to reinforce our policy priorities should be a major focus of U.S. economic strategy in Asia. Washington should also work to ensure that U.S. companies are insulated from pressure to support mercantilist practices, censorship, corruption, and labor or human rights abuses.
- *Work with allies and partners*: U.S. alliances and partnerships in the Asia Pacific can provide a powerful platform for advancing our economic as well as security interests in the region. They can help us spread high-standard rules and norms that benefit the United States and the broader region. In addition to regular mechanisms for consultation and cooperation, Washington should also look for opportunities to build issue-specific coalitions that advance our strategic goals in the region.

- *Make messaging a priority, not an afterthought*: The United States has a strong message in Asia: we have been a guarantor of peace and stability for decades, an important trade and investment partner, and a defender of shared values. Effective, consistent messaging is critical to success in Asia and should be integrated into policy from the outset, not left to after-action press releases. Clearly and consistently explaining to the American people and Congress the rationale for U.S. involvement in the Asia Pacific is also vital.

04

Recommendations

As we enter 2017 and a new administration, the United States needs a renewed prosperity agenda encompassing both sound domestic and international policies. To have a strong economy at home, we need to be successful in the Asia Pacific, the world's fastest-growing region. The region has enjoyed broad peace and prosperity, underpinned by U.S. investments in security partnerships, economic leadership, and support for universal values. The return on these investments has been impressive: expanded opportunities for American workers and businesses, a stable Asia helping to drive global economic growth, and support for American private sector leadership in innovation and frontier industries.

Nonetheless, the next administration can and must do better in the Asia Pacific, especially in our economic strategy. Though past administrations from both parties have done much to advance America's enduring interests in Asia, Washington has not done enough to combat unfair trade practices or to open foreign markets for American goods and services. Strengthening these efforts is central to the American interest and should be a key component of the next administration's prosperity agenda. Ultimately, more open, rules-based, competitive markets will not only serve the interests of the United States, but also advance sustainable growth, rising prosperity, and stability across the region.

Ensuring America's success in the Asia Pacific will also require major investments at home. Technological advancements in particular, and the rapid pace of globalization, have created new uncertainty and led to job displacement for many Americans. To restore the consensus in favor of robust U.S. economic involvement abroad, the new administration must make globalization work better for Americans. This means upgrading our infrastructure, overhauling our tax and regulatory regimes, investing in education and training programs that prepare American workers for the new economy, and funding assistance programs for displaced workers. These domestic policy choices are beyond the scope of this commission's work, but we acknowledge them as critical to the success of the strategy laid out here.

Together with a robust domestic agenda, the following recommendations for policy toward the Asia Pacific in the next administration are designed to provide a basis for continued effective and strategic U.S. economic leadership in this vital region:

1. Articulate a clear vision of the United States as a Pacific power

Presidential leadership is essential to mobilizing the U.S. government in support of a coherent and consistent strategy toward the Asia Pacific. The new president should immediately task his national security and economic team with developing a comprehensive strategy incorporating the objectives and principles in the previous chapter. He should also make an early and repeated case directly to the American people that the Asia Pacific is critical to the future of the United States. This will require highlighting the region in speeches to domestic audiences and working with local and congressional leaders to reinforce this message, as well as frequent, visible travel to the region by the president and cabinet members. The new administration must also listen; mechanisms for exchanging input with local leaders—especially governors and mayors—will be vital to both effective policymaking and public support for the strategy.

In addition to engaging Americans, the public articulation of this strategy must also speak to Asia. The next president must outline for U.S. allies and partners in the region a positive vision for the future of a fair, open, and rules-based trans-Pacific order. Public commitment to such a vision and an associated strategy is critical to restoring confidence in U.S. leadership in a region where uncertainty is growing and the balance of power rapidly shifting. This support will be critical to maintaining the regional economic and security order that has enabled the United States and the Asia Pacific to prosper over the past 70 years. In addition, the president and key administration officials must show up in the region early and often to reinforce U.S. commitment to regional leadership and collaboration.

Specific Implementation Steps

a. Include an explicit reference to America's role as a Pacific power in the president's inaugural address, and follow up with a major domestic policy speech on the importance of the Asia Pacific to America's future.

b. In the first year of the administration, prepare a Presidential Policy Directive (PPD) on U.S. strategy toward the region, with economics at the core, that will orient and align agency activities throughout the administration and best mesh with the way Asian countries view their own economic and security interests.

c. Begin planning early for the president's first trip to Asia and ensure annual—if not semiannual—presidential trips to the region as well as regular high-level interaction with Asian leaders at other international gatherings.

d. Strengthen the President's Export Council (PEC) and the Advisory Committee for Trade Policy and Negotiations (ACTPN) as forums for engaging the private sector and state and local officials, including governors and mayors, on U.S. foreign economic policy. Tangible outcomes are critical.

2. Complete TPP, and continue working to open markets and strengthen rules in the Asia Pacific

TPP has come under intense fire from many sides. Much of this criticism is based on a fundamental misunderstanding of what the agreement contains and what it is intended to do. The fact is that TPP advances U.S. interests in three tangible ways. First, by eliminating some 18,000 tariffs and expanding market access across the region, it creates U.S. export and job opportunities. Second, it creates new and updated rules for international trade and investment in areas critical to today's globalized economy, such as services, intellectual property protection, digital trade, labor and environment standards, regulatory transparency, competition policy, and state-owned enterprises. Finally, TPP is an essential complement to our military strategy in Asia, a region that views economics as the foundation of security. As Defense Secretary Ashton Carter remarked in 2015, "Passing TPP is as important to me as another aircraft carrier."

TPP is creating pressure on nonmember countries in Asia to improve their standards. Partners like South Korea and Taiwan have repeatedly expressed interest in joining TPP, while other major economies like China and Indonesia have shown interest in using the agreement to drive domestic reform. In addition, economic integration is viewed in Asia as synonymous with enhanced security, and TPP thereby helps reinforce the long-standing U.S. commitment to regional security.

For all these reasons, this commission strongly believes that it is critical that TPP—fixed as necessary—be ratified by the U.S. Congress. Withdrawal from TPP would have severe consequences. It would mean forgoing the commercial gains to the United States that would have come from more open markets and fairer competition in the Asia Pacific. It would mean a missed opportunity to write the rules that will govern trade in the world's fastest-growing region. It would cede the growth in Asian markets to our competitors, to the long-term disadvantage of both the U.S. economy and U.S. leadership.

There would also be strategic costs. Withdrawal would damage America's credibility as a partner in the Asia Pacific and elsewhere around the world and cede momentum in rulemaking to other nations, most notably China, that do not share our values or interests in important areas. It would undoubtedly erode the United States' near-term influence in the Asia Pacific.

In addition to implementing the TPP, the new administration should work with America's allies and partners to further advance U.S. economic interests in the world's most dynamic region. It should ensure that the TPP rules on services, where the U.S. economy has important comparative advantages, are embedded in a strong plurilateral Trade in Services Agreement (TiSA). It should accelerate the negotiation of bilateral investment agreements with key Asian partners. As a matter of law and principle, the United States already provides fair treatment to foreign firms operating on American soil; investment agreements provide a critical mechanism for guaranteeing that American firms operating abroad receive the same high standard of treatment.

The new administration should also redouble its involvement in APEC. While often undervalued, APEC has several features that make it fertile ground for creative U.S. economic diplomacy in pursuit of broader strategic interests. First, it is anchored by an annual leaders' meeting, which provides an important venue for the U.S. president to meet with his Asia-Pacific counterparts and press our economic interests. Second, with Vietnam as chair of APEC in 2017, the United States has a proactive and strategically important country to partner with. Third, Taiwan is a member of APEC—one of the only regional institutions in which it participates. A reinvigorated APEC could help address Taiwan's growing economic isolation as it remains excluded from the region's rapidly expanding regional free trade network.

Meanwhile, Washington policymakers should draw political and policy lessons from the recent TPP experience. This includes the need to do more to ensure that the benefits of trade and international engagement are delivered to all Americans, as well as to make the investments at home needed to help prepare businesses and workers for the new global economy.

There are also positive lessons in the successful TPP approach to strategic economic policymaking that created incentives for other countries in the region to join the United States in opening markets and updating the rules of international trade and investment. This could be applied to other areas of economic policy, such as setting high standards for infrastructure investment, as well as for health, energy, and other services. Government procurement is another area where creative U.S. leadership could help remove existing roadblocks and create new opportunities to advance high standards.

Specific Implementation Steps

a. Engage with trading partners to remedy TPP as needed, and then prepare the ground with Congress, industry, and the American public for ratification and vigorous enforcement of TPP.

b. Conclude a strong TiSA agreement and expand it to other key trading partners.

c. Conclude high-standard investment agreements with non-TPP economies, including China, India, and Indonesia.

d. Step up work in APEC to promote high standards for trade and investment and build capacity in the region's less-developed economies.

e. Revive multilateral rulemaking on government procurement by proposing, as a first step, an agreement on transparency in government procurement separate from market access obligations, with the latter to follow.

3. Take action to ensure that the U.S.-China relationship is mutually beneficial

The U.S.-China economic relationship is one of the most important in the world, shaping the prospects for global economic growth and financial stability. A successful U.S. economic strategy in the Asia-Pacific region depends on ensuring a strong and mutually beneficial relationship with China. Growing trade and investment between the United States and China over the past four decades has had broad benefits for both sides (though as recent research has shown, not without disruption).[1] China's implementation of plans to rebalance its economy toward greater consumption and services will create enormous demand for goods and services that, all things being equal, U.S. firms are well positioned to meet. Moreover, growth of Chinese direct investment in the United States is generally welcome as supporting American jobs and growth.

However, the U.S.-China relationship today is out of balance. Impediments to U.S. companies' freely serving the Chinese market are growing and creating new bilateral friction at the industry and policy level. These impediments reflect government policy choices by Beijing rather than the natural development of the economy. China continues to place equity ownership limitations and other investment restrictions on foreign firms' operation in certain sectors. Recent legislation and pending laws, including those on national security, foreign nongovernmental organizations (NGOs), cybersecurity, and the Internet, have created new uncertainty and discrimination in the operating environment for foreign firms. Implementation of existing legislation, such as the Anti-Monopoly Law, has also been discrimination in many cases. A raft of guidelines, regulations, and normative documents underscore China's intent to pursue indigenization across industry sectors, particularly with respect to IP and technology-intensive industries. Long-range planning documents, such as the 13th Five-Year Plan and Made in China 2025, offer explicit statements of Beijing's intent to indigenize the "commanding heights" of the innovation economy.

As a result of these inhospitable policies and practices in China, the decades-old U.S. strategy of engaging with China to pull it more deeply into the global rules-based order, encouraging cooperation where possible while managing competition, faces a serious challenge. China's domestic political landscape and its economic and foreign policy objectives have evolved in ways that create new and serious uncertainties that demand more sophisticated strategies by the U.S. private sector and government.

The United States has a range of tools with which to pursue a mutually beneficial U.S.-China economic relationship. The new administration must be willing to respond forcefully to Chinese practices that harm U.S. interests and to consider approaches that go beyond merely asking China to reduce its sweeping trade and investment barriers. For example, intellectual property theft costs the U.S. economy in excess of $300 billion per year, with the majority of this attributed to China.[2] The next administration should immediately demonstrate its strong commitment to protecting American IP by appointing the new Chief Innovation and IP Negotiator authorized by Congress in 2016 and solicit private-sector advice to establish priorities. In addition, the administration should use and expand its toolkit to ensure that it can respond forcefully to cyber theft and foreign products benefitting from forced technology transfer.

1. David H. Autor, David Dorn, and Gordon H. Hanson, *The China Shock: Learning from Labor Market Adjustment to Large Changes in Trade*, Working Paper No. 21906 (Cambridge, MA: National Bureau of Economic Research, January 2016), http://www.nber.org/papers/w21906.pdf.

2. IP Commission (IPC), *The Report of the Commission on the Theft of the American Intellectual Property* (Seattle, WA: National Bureau of Asian Research, May 2013), http://www.ipcommission.org/report/ip_commission_report_052213.pdf.

The new administration should also look for opportunities to advance American interests through negotiations. Conclusion of a high-standard and enforceable investment agreement represents the most significant opportunity to enhance protections for U.S. companies against discrimination, market access barriers, and idiosyncratic enforcement of law. To the extent Beijing sees such an agreement as a way of keeping the U.S. market open to Chinese investors, it could be useful leverage for the next administration in insisting on reciprocal treatment for U.S. investors in China.

These are only recommended first steps; they must be part of a broader strategy through which Washington demonstrates greater willingness to prevent China's actions from harming U.S. interests and to ensure that Beijing is held accountable to its international obligations and responsibilities. The new president should communicate this resolve early on and directly to the Chinese president.

Meanwhile, regular channels of communication between Washington and Beijing need to be streamlined and improved. Both the Strategic & Economic Dialogue (S&ED), the principal vehicle for high-level engagement over the past decade, and the Joint Commission on Commerce and Trade (JCCT), the main forum for dialogue on commercial issues, have become unwieldy and of diminished utility in delivering concrete, meaningful progress on issues of critical importance. The new president should ensure high-level political attention to key opportunities and challenges through small, high-level forums to achieve meaningful results.

Specific Implementation Steps

a. In an early call with the Chinese president, President Trump should make clear that the incoming administration is determined to have a mutually beneficial relationship with China, will identify areas for potential cooperation as well as priority areas of concern, and will take forceful action to defend U.S. security and economic interests. The president should stress that talk will not substitute for the further reform and opening that will be required if the United States and China are to maintain productive relations.

b. In that first official presidential call, propose the transformation of the S&ED and JCCT through a new framework for high-level dialogue on major issues in the U.S.-China relationship that includes the following elements:

    i. Annual "Sunnylands-style" (i.e., extended and informal) summits between the two leaders that establish bilateral priorities and goals, and commitment to review progress on these goals on a regular basis.

    ii. Small, elevated forums in relevant functional areas between the actual decisionmakers in the two systems designated by the two leaders. For example, the U.S. treasury secretary and the director of the Chinese Communist Party's Finance and Economics Leading Small Group would lead the resolution of macroeconomic, financial, and related issues.

    iii. A regular, informal channel between the national security adviser and the director of the National Economic Council (NEC)—the U.S. president's top foreign policy and economic advisers, respectively—with the closest and most senior advisers to the Chinese president on priorities in the U.S.-China relationship and the timeline for action. This 2x2 group should meet in person at least twice a year and have virtual exchanges on an ad hoc basis as issues arise.

c. Use existing U.S. laws, such as the Trade Act of 1974 (as amended), to more actively investigate Chinese unfair trade and investment practices and develop action plans to address those practices. Allocate sufficient resources to ensure robust enforcement of existing trade laws. Work with Congress to consider new legal tools to support U.S. economic interests.

d. Seek to conclude a high-standard investment agreement with China that provides robust protections from discriminatory policies for U.S. companies operating in the Chinese market and vastly opens China's market to U.S. investment in both nature and scope, as provided in the United States. Continue to monitor Chinese FDI inflows and seek to maximize the benefits of these investments while insisting on reciprocal treatment of U.S. investment and investors in China.

e. Convene a process for regular engagement of stakeholders in the private sector and civil society to assess the state of the U.S.-China relationship, with specific attention to issues inconsistent with mutually beneficial economic relations. Issue an annual public report summarizing the findings of this process and benchmarking against the previous year.

4. Take action to maintain U.S. technological leadership

The United States is a global technology leader and the world's largest spender on research and development activities. Maintaining American technological preeminence is critically important to ensuring good, high-paying jobs for U.S. workers, as well as strengthening U.S. national security. IP-intensive industries account for over 60 percent of U.S. merchandise exports, and wages in IP-intensive industries average more than 40 percent above those in other private industries.[3] American leadership in technology and innovation is vital to economic growth and dynamism and helps to attract foreign investment, researchers, and students. It also makes the United States and U.S. companies high-value targets for technology acquisition and exfiltration efforts, both legal and illegal. Estimates suggest that IP theft—including cyber-enabled theft—costs the United States at least $300 billion per year.

Maintaining U.S. technological preeminence is first and foremost a function of making the right investments at home. This means adequate spending on research and development (R&D), education, and infrastructure, as well as promoting appropriate legal regimes and cultural institutions. It also means targeted public-sector investments in innovation through proven mechanisms such as the Defense Advanced Research Projects Agency, National Institute of Standards and Technology, and National Institutes of Health, and developing new channels for engaging

3. U.S. International Trade Commission, "USITC Releases Report Concerning the Likely Impact of the Trans-Pacific Partnership (TPP) Agreement," news release, May 18, 2016, https://www.usitc.gov/press_room/news_release/2016/er0518ll597.htm.

innovators and investing federal funds throughout the domestic innovation ecosystem. Basic research relevant to frontier industries—such as biotechnology, nanotechnology, advanced materials, robotics, artificial intelligence, and renewable energy—deserves special attention in this regard. At present, federal spending on research and development as a share of total government outlays is at its lowest level since 1968 and, as a percentage of GDP, has fallen more than a third since the late 1970s.[4] This is a threat to U.S. technology preeminence and the U.S. economy.

Maintaining America's technological edge also requires facilitating U.S. companies' activities abroad. One vital area for improvement is international standards setting. Standards, as well as governmental and private standards-setting organizations such as the International Telecommunication Union (ITU), the Internet Corporation for Assigned Names and Numbers (ICANN), the Society for Worldwide Interbank Financial Telecommunication (SWIFT), and the Clearing House Interbank Payments System (CHIPS), play an often underappreciated role in enhancing (or reducing) economic efficiency. The U.S. private sector has a proven track record of developing fair, transparent, and efficient standards, but the U.S. government is not always effective in supporting their internationalization or avoiding the imposition by foreign countries of unique and discriminatory national standards. Doing more in these areas would have positive effects for U.S. competitiveness and leadership in frontier industries, as well as produce efficiency gains for the global economy.

Preventing restrictions on cross-border data flows, including data localization requirements, should also be a priority. Restrictions on the free flow of data and onerous localization requirements not only undermine the competitive advantage of leading U.S. companies, they often fail to advance the stated policy objectives of the governments that impose them. To prevent these restrictions and requirements from proliferating, the next administration must make it a priority to push for openness in relevant negotiations and international forums, while also working with the private sector to help educate partner countries on the benefits of openness.

In addition, the United States must change the cost-benefit calculation for IP theft by both state and private actors and do a better job of protecting U.S. technology assets. This requires specific actions, including more robust enforcement of existing laws and regulations and updating the U.S. legal regime regarding cyber-enabled theft of IP.

Specific Implementation Steps

a. Develop a pro-innovation strategy at home that includes investment in infrastructure and education, tax and regulatory reform, and increased federal investment in R&D.

b. Actively promote the adoption of standards developed or preferred by the U.S. private sector in regional organizations and international institutions, and ensure effective representation of the United States in international standards-setting bodies.

---

4. Massachusetts Institute of Technology, "The Future Postponed," accessed October 2016, http://www.futurepostponed.org.

c. Strengthen and build on APEC members' commitment to existing APEC investment and innovation principles,[5] and work through APEC and other relevant forums to root out localization requirements and restrictions on cross-border data flows.

d. Implement key recommendations of the 2013 IP Commission Report[6] (the Huntsman-Blair report), among others:

   i. Require the Securities and Exchange Commission to judge whether companies' use of stolen IP is a material condition that ought to be publicly reported.

   ii. Greatly expand the number of green cards available to foreign students who earn science, technology, engineering, and mathematics degrees in American universities and who have a job offer in their field upon graduation.

   iii. Establish a quick-response capability to sequester imported goods that incorporate stolen or pirated materials or were made with a business process that includes illegally procured intellectual property, strengthening the existing Section 337 process of the Tariff Act of 1930.

e. Use Executive Order 13694 to aggressively deter cyber-enabled theft of American IP. This provision, issued by President Obama in 2015, authorizes the government to sanction individuals and entities that conduct cyber-enabled activities that threaten U.S. national security, foreign policy, economic health, or financial stability.

5. Bring U.S. strengths to the infrastructure push across Asia

In recent years, there has been a rush among regional powers to shape Asia's connectivity infrastructure, including both hard infrastructure (e.g., roads and rails, energy pipelines, and information and communications technology links) and soft infrastructure (e.g., customs procedures). Through the AIIB and OBOR, China has been the most prominent actor in this space, though other countries such as Japan, South Korea, and India have their own visions for the region. Washington currently does not have a coherent strategy for participating in the infrastructure push in Asia. The incoming administration should develop such a strategy, leading with U.S. strengths: commitment to the rule of law, high standards, transparency, and world-leading companies that know how to prepare, finance, and execute infrastructure projects.

The United States and Asia both benefit from connectivity infrastructure that is of high quality and sustainable and supports trade. For the United States, the construction of quality infrastructure in Asia offers commercial opportunities for U.S. companies, while access to this infrastructure is important to the competitiveness of many other U.S. businesses. For the region, addressing major infrastructure gaps is vital to ensuring sustained and sustainable economic development and the growth of a resilient middle class. For all countries, disaster-resilient infrastructure is

---

5. APEC, "APEC Non-Binding Investment Principles," news release, November 1994, http://www.apec.org/Press/News-Releases/2010/~/media/965E37FDA6D848B4A0350D68D2A4BE1C.ashx.

6. IPC, *The Report of the Commission on the Theft of the American Intellectual Property.*

essential to reducing the impact of natural disasters. Whether infrastructure is built according to high standards will have consequences that range from debt sustainability to social stability. All of this will have an impact on the strategic environment in Asia.

The region can build the infrastructure it needs to continue to grow robustly only if it finds a way to more effectively mobilize *private* long-term capital to finance it, either from domestic savings or externally. The United States should help the region deepen and broaden capital markets in Asia that supply that long-term capital and work with like-minded countries to better prepare and market public-private partnerships. As a starting point, Washington should work with partners to define a set of principles for infrastructure investment—including lifecycle-cost-based procurement, natural-disaster resilience, environmental and social safeguards, and debt sustainability—that would provide greater certainty about the viability of projects and help mobilize private capital to fund infrastructure in the region. Washington should also work with multilateral development banks (MDBs), including the World Bank, ADB, and AIIB, and other partners to build out a coordinated blueprint for regional connectivity. It should look for opportunities to better coordinate the activities of the dozens of project preparation facilities (PPFs) already active in the region, including those most recently established by China under the auspices of the AIIB.

At the same time, the next administration needs to do a better job of supporting U.S. companies abroad so that they are able to compete against often heavily subsidized competitors from other countries, particularly China. To ensure that U.S.-headquartered businesses are able to maintain sufficient global economies of scale, it is essential that the U.S. government expand the dollar value and variety of export financing and investment guarantee mechanisms available through U.S. government agencies such as the Export-Import Bank (Ex-Im) and the Overseas Private Investment Corporation (OPIC). (Ex-Im funding is important not just for infrastructure-related opportunities but to support U.S. exports of high-value products and services such as airplanes and turbines.) Technical-assistance efforts, such as helping countries to understand the importance of considering lifecycle costs in infrastructure procurement, can help improve the competitive position of U.S. companies. However, absent associated financing, high-quality U.S. products may remain beyond the fiscal resources of recipient countries.

Specific Implementation Steps

a. Develop a set of principles for governing infrastructure investment that promote transparency, regulatory certainty, and a level playing field for U.S. business. Work with partners to refine and gain acceptance for these principles across the Asia Pacific.

b. Win support for MDBs to design a comprehensive regional infrastructure blueprint based on these principles.

c. Within this plan, work with the World Bank, ADB, AIIB, and national governments to designate priority projects as a means of coordinating partners and improving project viability, including through creation of PPFs independent from governments that can work with national officials to prepare and seek funding for specific projects.

d. Increase infrastructure-related technical assistance through the U.S. Treasury Department, USAID, and Trade and Development Agency (USTDA). Enhance collaboration with the private sector to run courses on procurement excellence and other topics necessary to build a more informed customer base.

e. Benchmark current U.S. export-support efforts against regional commercial competitors (including allies) and significantly expand the resources and product offerings of the Ex-Im and OPIC to support the competitiveness of U.S. products and services.

f. Build on the U.S.-ASEAN Connect initiative,[7] launched at Sunnylands in February 2016, by expanding the number of one-stop-shop centers across Southeast Asia to better coordinate U.S. economic engagement on infrastructure, information and communications technology (ICT), and energy, and to connect more entrepreneurs, investors, and businesses with each other.

6. Update and uphold the Asia-Pacific economic architecture

Successive U.S. administrations have invested in building and sustaining Asia-Pacific economic institutions. These institutions, such as APEC and the ADB, have played important roles in promoting regional economic integration, liberalization, and habits of cooperation. They have also been important sources of leverage for Washington in strengthening trans-Pacific (rather than Asia-only) patterns of economic exchange, support the diffusion of high standards, and further embed the United States in the region. Today the U.S.-led order is facing greater challenge than at any time since World War II. The motivations driving nations such as China to invest in new institutions range from dissatisfaction with voting arrangements in existing institutions to fundamental disagreements over who should lead and what standards should prevail.

The United States has an interest in updating and upholding a regional economic order that reflects both U.S. priorities and shared values with our partners, such as openness and fairness. Rather than retrenchment, the current environment calls for smart policies to adjust and strengthen the existing order and further support high-standard economic integration. As recommended in the Atlantic Council's 2015 report *Shaping the Asia-Pacific Future*,[8] Washington should take action to enhance the resources and practices of the ADB and take other steps to strengthen regional institutions. In particular, the United States should work with the ADB to explore how it can better leverage its funding to "crowd in" long-term institutional investor capital for Asian infrastructure projects. In addition, it should encourage a concurrent review of best practices and standards at major development institutions (such as for infrastructure investment) to help promote more consistent approaches across different organizations. At the same time, in recognition of Asians' desire for more ownership of regional economic architecture, the new administration should consider some form of U.S. participation in the AIIB.

---

7. White House Office of the Press Secretary, "Strategic Partners for Sustainable and Innovative Economic Growth Connect Represents the Next Chapter in the U.S.-ASEAN Economic Relationship," fact sheet, September 8, 2016, https://www.whitehouse.gov/the-press-office/2016/09/08/fact-sheet-us-asean-connect.

8. Olin Wethington and Robert A. Manning, *Shaping the Asia-Pacific Future: Strengthening the Institutional Architecture for an Open, Rules-Based Economic Order* (Washington, DC: Atlantic Council, 2015), http://www.atlanticcouncil.org/images/publications/Shaping_AP_Future_Digital.pdf.

The new administration should also work to strengthen APEC. Among other things, it should find ways to enhance the role of APEC's Policy Support Unit (PSU). This step would support U.S. and regional interests by enhancing the scope and quality of available economic data and establishing best practices. The administration should also put additional emphasis on APEC working groups in priority areas, such as health, energy, and ICT. At the same time, Washington should step up its engagement with ASEAN-centered institutions and participate more fully in the economic dimensions of ASEAN cooperation.

Specific Implementation Steps

a. Sustain high-level participation in key regional forums, including regular participation by the president at the EAS, APEC, and U.S.-ASEAN summits.

b. Invite ASEAN leaders to the United States in 2017 for a U.S.-ASEAN summit, building on the gains made at the 2016 Sunnylands summit.

c. Review and adopt key recommendations on institutional reform in the Atlantic Council's 2015 *Shaping the Asia-Pacific Future* report.

d. As part of an overall effort to reinvigorate APEC, work to strengthen the PSU's efforts to improve regional data quality and monitoring and spread best practices. Promote the PSU as an incubator for regional standard-setting efforts and a hub for private-sector engagement on standard setting.

e. Building on APEC's vital role in encouraging voluntary cooperation and best practices, work with allies and partners to improve the level of cybersecurity awareness across the region. Promoting sound understanding of cybersecurity is critical to building support for the multi-stakeholder model of Internet governance and other U.S. priorities, such as ensuring the free flow of data.

f. Reinforce the underpinnings of regional institutions and strengthen U.S. educational and ideational linkages with Asia by promoting U.S.-style education centers in the region (such as Fulbright University Vietnam) and encouraging greater linkages between U.S. and regional policy institutions (such as think tanks).

g. Continue to promote greater regional financial integration by supporting stronger domestic capital markets in ASEAN countries.

7. Work with Congress to rebuild U.S. leverage and fully resource U.S. priorities in Asia

Past congressional action has been critical to providing the executive branch with the resources and leverage to pursue a robust foreign policy agenda in the Asia Pacific. These assets have been diminished in recent years, leaving U.S. priorities in Asia badly under-resourced. The resources for diplomatic and development efforts that the United States currently invests in East Asia are the lowest of any region, while current trade laws may not be adequate—or adequately enforced—to advance U.S. interests in today's complex Asia-Pacific setting.

As a first step, the next administration should conduct a review to assess the adequacy of current spending levels (including spending on personnel) and identify whether and where additional investments are needed. The administration should also do an inventory of measures available under current law to address unfair practices identified in reports such as the annual Special 301 Report on Intellectual Property Rights (IPR) and the National Trade Estimates Report on Foreign Trade Barriers. Having conducted this review, the administration should request that Congress either provide specific additional authorities to augment U.S. leverage and/or authorize greater resources for regulatory enforcement.

The administration should also seek increased congressional funding for programs that better leverage the unique strengths of the U.S. private sector and civil society. These include programs, such as the Franklin Fellowship, that encourage personnel exchange between the public and private sectors, and programs that promote student and visitor exchanges with Asia, including the Fulbright program and the State Department's International Visitor Leadership Program (IVLP). Ensuring that the U.S. government has access to the skills and energy of America's best and brightest, and that the best and brightest in Asia have opportunities to engage with their American counterparts, presents a vital opportunity to improve the quality of policy and the long-term trajectory of U.S. relationships in Asia.

Specific Implementation Steps

a. Request that Congress establish a high-level, bipartisan advisory group, including elected officials from local governments, members of Congress, and leading technical experts on economics, trade, security, global value chains, and technology, to investigate and make recommendations for improving U.S. economic intelligence and analytical capabilities in the Asia Pacific.

b. Conduct a review of U.S. legal authorities for responding to IP theft, market access barriers, and related impediments, as well as a review of resources for enforcement, and enhance both as appropriate.

c. Work with Congress to develop fully resourced programs to deter unfair competition and curb market-distorting policies in the region.

d. Direct the Government Accountability Office (GAO) to assess whether U.S. Customs and Border Patrol (CBP) is effectively enforcing existing legislation, such as on human rights, the environment, forced labor, and inspections of products that violate IPR and product safety standards.

e. Expand funding for the hiring of Asia specialists, including those with language capability, in the Departments of State, Treasury, Commerce, and the Office of the U.S. Trade Representative (USTR) and the intelligence community.

f. Increase the number and range of fellowships (such as the Franklin Fellowships) for individuals from the private sector to transition into the public sector (and vice versa), to help with public-private information sharing.

g. Increase funding levels for civil society exchange programs active in Asia, especially the IVLP, and set aside more funding for scholarship programs aimed at training next-generation leaders from less-developed countries in Asia.

8. Build an effective interagency Asia economic team coordinated by the White House

The apparatus of U.S. policymaking is not designed to support a comprehensive and effective Asia economic strategy. The National Security Council (NSC) was established during the Cold War when the principal challenges facing the United States were not economic and not centered in Asia. The NEC, established during the Clinton administration to coordinate all U.S. economic policymaking, international and domestic, has evolved to become a body principally focused on domestic policy coordination. In the twenty-first century, economics must play an enhanced role in the shaping and implementation of national security strategy, and domestic and international policy must be better integrated. In particular, the White House structure and culture should reflect the importance of economic tools in a comprehensive strategy toward the Asia region. To this end, there should be one very senior official, reporting to both the national security adviser and the director of the NEC, who is responsible for overseeing Asian economic policy. At present, that responsibility often falls in the cracks between the senior director for Asia, the deputy national security adviser for international economics, and the NEC.

This lack of coordination extends to international economic policy efforts more generally, which are highly disaggregated, often work in silos, and are sometimes at odds with each other. The White House needs better coordination across the government, particularly with respect to Asia. Two changes are of particular importance. First, the White House has become increasingly involved in operational policy implementation, stifling agency initiative, rather than playing its more appropriate role as overall policy coordinator. Second, the international economic policy of the United States cannot be made in a vacuum; the national security establishment—including the Department of Defense—has an important role to play and should be better integrated into the process.

White House outreach and consultation with various stakeholders—Congress, the private sector, and state and local governments—are also critical. The next administration must revitalize mechanisms for engaging with these stakeholders. This should be done not only as a means for the White House to seek support for its positions, but in order to solicit feedback, aggregate information, and generate locally informed policy proposals through which Washington can effectively advance the interests of all Americans.

Finally, economic and commercial officers at U.S. embassies must be directed specifically to advocate for U.S. strategic interests in Asia and make value-added contributions to Washington policymaking. They tend to report on local developments and other routine activities rather than providing value-added insights that would make for better policy. Moreover, they tend to be overwhelmingly focused on bilateral relationships and miss opportunities for inter-Asian, cross-border initiatives, including efforts that would boost trans-Pacific economic integration.

Specific Implementation Steps

a. Designate the national security adviser and the head of the NEC as the primary officials responsible for implementation of the Presidential Policy Directive on U.S. Asia-Pacific strategy (see recommendation 1b), including its economic dimensions.

b. Designate a single senior official, reporting directly to both the national security adviser and the NEC director, as responsible for overseeing and coordinating U.S. economic strategy toward Asia.

c. Establish a standing interagency committee chaired by this official that designs and implements Asia economic strategy, pulling in key Asia and economic policy officials from across government, including national security agencies, as well as implementing agencies, such as Ex-Im and OPIC. Outreach to key stakeholders—including Congress, local governments, and the private sector—should be a priority for this group.

d. Reduce reporting and other routine requirements for State and Commerce officers at post, particularly in the Asia-Pacific region, and better channel their energies toward collaboration and value-added contributions to strategic economic policymaking.

About the Commissioners

COMMISSION COCHAIRS

Charlene Barshefsky has had a distinguished career in law and public service. As senior international partner at WilmerHale, Ambassador Barshefsky represents multinational corporations and private equity firms in global markets, including negotiations with foreign governments. Prior to this, she served as the United States trade representative (1997–2001). As a member of President Bill Clinton's cabinet, she was responsible for the formulation of U.S. trade policy and the negotiation of hundreds of complex trade and investment agreements, including China's World Trade Organization (WTO) agreement, and global agreements in the financial services, telecommunications, high-tech products and cyberspace.

Evan G. Greenberg is one of America's leading insurance executives. He is the chairman and CEO of Chubb Limited and Chubb Group (formerly ACE Limited and ACE Group). He sits on the CSIS Board of Trustees, and other affiliations include vice chairman of the National Committee on U.S.-China Relations, and board member of the U.S.-China Business Council.

Jon M. Huntsman Jr. has served in each of the past five presidential administrations, beginning with the Reagan administration. He is currently the chairman of the Atlantic Council and co-chairman of No Labels. During his career in public service, he has served as U.S. ambassador to China and to Singapore, Deputy United States Trade Representative, and was twice elected governor of Utah.

COMMISSIONERS

Timothy Adams is currently president and CEO of the Institute of International Finance. His career spans the public and private sector. He previously served as undersecretary of the treasury for international affairs (2005–2007) and as chief of staff to two former treasury secretaries, and as managing director of The Lindsey Group.

Richard L. Armitage has had a distinguished career in public service, most recently as deputy secretary of state (2001–2005). He was also assistant secretary of defense for international security affairs (1983–1989). A decorated Vietnam veteran, Secretary Armitage is president of Armitage International and sits on the CSIS Board of Trustees.

Gary Baumgartner is the founder and chairman of GJB Corp., an equity research and investment firm focused on targeting deep value investments. He is a global leader in the energy oil industry, having spent the last forty years emphasizing downstream technology worldwide. He is cofounder of International Alliance Group (IAG), which has delivered that technology to over 35 countries.

Karan Bhatia is vice president and senior counsel, global government affairs and policy, for General Electric. In addition to his substantial private-sector experience, he has held senior roles in the Department of Commerce and Department of Transportation and served as deputy United States trade representative in the George W. Bush administration (2005–2007).

Gary Edson is principal of Civic Enterprises. He is a White House veteran and a recognized leader in global development. He has served in senior roles in the Department of State, the Office of the U.S. Trade Representative, and the White House, including as deputy national security adviser, deputy national economic adviser, and deputy assistant to the president for international economic affairs (2001–2004).

Anne Finucane is vice chairman at Bank of America and a member of the board's executive management team. She is responsible for the strategic positioning of Bank of America and leads the company's Environmental, Social, and Governance (ESG) efforts. In addition, she oversees public policy, customer research and analytics, global marketing, and communications. She is active in public service, serving on numerous corporate and nonprofit boards.

Stephen W. Green has had a distinguished career in the energy sector. He currently serves as president of Chevron Asia Pacific Exploration and Production Company. Before joining Chevron, he held numerous senior roles with Unocal, including as chief executive officer of Unocal Thailand, Ltd.

Reed Hundt is an adviser to the Washington, D.C. law firm Covington, the founder and chief executive officer of the Coalition for Green Capital, and a member of various boards, including Intel. He was chairman of the Federal Communications Commission (1993–1997) and has written four books, including *In China's Shadow: The Crisis of American Entrepreneurship* (New Haven, CT: Yale University Press, 2006).

Rod Hunter is a partner at Baker McKenzie. He served as senior director for international economics at the White House's National Security Council under President George W. Bush.

Charles Lake is president of Aflac International, Aflac Japan. He is also President Emeritus of the American Chamber of Commerce in Japan and currently sits on nonprofit boards, including the Peterson Institute for International Economics, Coalition of Service Industries, and U.S.-Japan Business Council. He is an independent outside director on publicly listed company boards.

J. Stapleton Roy is distinguished scholar and founding director emeritus of the Kissinger Institute on China and the United States at the Woodrow Wilson Center. He is an accomplished diplomat, whose assignments with the U.S. Department of State included tours as ambassador to Singapore, China, and Indonesia, and as assistant secretary for intelligence and research.

Kathleen Stephens was a U.S. foreign service officer for over 30 years, serving in numerous senior diplomacy roles, including as U.S. ambassador to South Korea (2008–2011), acting under secretary of state for public diplomacy and public affairs, and as United States chargé d'affaires to India (2014). She is currently a distinguished fellow at Stanford University.

Mona Sutphen is a partner with Macro Advisory Partners and a member of the President's Intelligence Advisory Board. She served as White House deputy chief of staff for policy (2009–2011) and in the U.S. foreign service (1991–2000), serving in the interim as managing director at Stonebridge International.

Christopher Townsend is president of MetLife's Asia region and a member of the company's executive group. His career in the insurance industry spans over twenty-five years, during which he has held a range of senior executive positions helping organizations successfully drive their business and growth strategies in Asia.

Laura D'Andrea Tyson has had a distinguished career in the public sector and academia. She served as the first female chairman of the White House Council of Economic Advisers (1933–1995) and as Director of the National Economic Council (1995–1996). She is a distinguished professor at the Berkeley Haas School of Business and previously served as its dean.

About the Project Directors and Staff

PROJECT DIRECTORS

Matthew P. Goodman is senior adviser for Asian economics and holds the William E. Simon Chair in Political Economy at CSIS. He has served twice in senior positions on the White House National Security Council staff, as well as in the Department of Treasury and the Department of State. His private-sector experience includes work at Goldman Sachs and Albright Stonebridge Group. He currently serves as chairman of the board of trustees of the Japan-America Society of Washington.

Scott Miller is a senior adviser and holds the William M. Scholl Chair in International Business at CSIS. He was previously director for global trade policy at Procter & Gamble (1997–2012) and has been a key contributor to U.S. international trade and investment policy for many years, participating in trade and investment advisory committees at the Department of State, Department of Commerce, and the Office of the U.S. Trade Representative.

Amy E. Searight is senior adviser and director of the Southeast Asia Program at CSIS. Her career has spanned defense, diplomacy, development, and economics in both government and academia. Most recently, she served in the Department of Defense as deputy assistant secretary of defense for South and Southeast Asia (2014–2016) and previously served in senior roles at USAID and the State Department. Her past academic affiliations have included George Washington, Northwestern, and Harvard universities.

PROJECT STAFF

Benjamin Contreras
Program Manager, Southeast Asia Program

Shannon Hayden
Associate Director, Southeast Asia Program

Grace Hearty
Former Associate Director, Simon Chair in Political Economy

Murray Hiebert
Senior Fellow and Deputy Director, Southeast Asia Program

Elizabeth Keller
Research Assistant and Program Coordinator, Simon Chair in Political Economy

Phuong Nguyen
Former Associate Fellow, Southeast Asia Program

David A. Parker
Associate Fellow, Simon Chair in Political Economy

Daniel Remler
Research Assistant, Simon Chair in Political Economy

Kathleen Rustici
Former Associate Director, Southeast Asia Program

Daniel G. Sofio
Research Assistant, Scholl Chair in International Business

INTERNS

Lesley Brock
Michelle Jiyoung Han
Ethan Rogers
Crystal Styron
Khine Thant Su
Brandon Whitehill

www.ingramcontent.com/pod-product-compliance
Ingram Content Group UK Ltd.
Pitfield, Milton Keynes, MK11 3LW, UK
UKHW051418150926
475561UK00005B/228

9 781442 279766